HE LED ALL THE WAY

Dorothy Lord Bausum Evans

Dorothy Lord Bausum Evans
Romans 8:28

DEDICATION

This book is dedicated to my beloved husband,
Bobby Dale Evans,
who has unconditionally loved me for 50 years
and untiringly encouraged me to write this story,

and

to our precious children
who have each read
and approved
this accounting of God's leading
in our family's life.

CONTENTS

Author's Word
Glossary
Prologue
The First Seven Years
The Second Seven Years
The Third Seven Years
The Fourth Seven Years
Five Times Seven Years
Epilogue
Appendix
   A Delightful Inheritance
   Bausum – Malaya
   Lord – China
   Bausum/Lord – China
   Bausum/Lord – America
   Bausum – China
   Family Trees
   Maps

AUTHOR'S WORD

Many people have told me, "Write the story of your life." Some might think me presumptuous for doing this as if I think I am someone special. Conversely, seeing the hand of God moving throughout the life of my family, is it not my obligation to write this story?

I have wrestled with this question because I DO have a story to tell, not only of MY life, but that of three generations of missionaries before me on my father's side of the family. The more I thought about the issue the more I realized that NOT to write the entire story would be to neglect a powerful testimony to God's leading. He has led across oceans, countries, and time, not only in my own life but also in the life of my family.

It was, then, with trembling hand and determined heart that I sat down at my computer to write the amazing story of the Bausum and Lord families, beginning with my great-grandfathers and coming down to my own generation. My desire is not to focus on the various characters that parade across the pages of this book but to call the reader's attention to how God led members of this family, over the past almost 200 years, to carry out His Great Commission.

As I wrote this story, always in my heart was my favorite hymn that so beautifully declares the testimony of these four generations of missionaries:

All the way my Savior leads me; What have I to ask beside?
Can I doubt His tender mercy, Who through life has been my guide?
Heav'nly peace, divinest comfort, Here by faith in Him to dwell!
For I know whate'er befalls me, Jesus doeth all things well.

All the way my Savior leads me; Cheers each winding path I tread,
Gives me grace for ev'ry trial, Feeds me with the living bread;
Tho' my weary steps may falter, And my soul athirst may be,
Gushing from the Rock before me, Lo! a spring of joy I see.

All the way my Savior leads me; Oh, the fullness of His love!
Perfect rest to me is promised In my Father's house above:
When my spirit, clothed immortal, Wings its flight to realms of day,
This my song thro' endless ages; Jesus led me all the way.

Fanny J. Crosby, 1820-1915

Dorothy Lord Bausum Evans
Independence, Missouri
bdevans@comcast.net
2007

GLOSSARY

Amah – a hired helper/maid in an Asian home
Bahasa Malaysia (BM) – national language of Malaysia; also called Malay
Borneo – Third largest island in the world; located in Southeast Asia
Brig – guardhouse/prison on a ship
Brunei Darussalam – independent nation on northwest coast of Borneo
BSB - Bandar Seri Begawan (capital of Brunei Darussalam)
Cantonese – Chinese dialect native to Guangdong, China
Compound – a walled in area with a number of buildings
Customs – government agency to examine imported items to determine taxes due
Dyak – aboriginal peoples living in the interior of Borneo
East Coast – the eastern coast of the Malay Peninsula
FMB – Foreign Mission Board (now IMB)
Georgetown – main city on island of Penang
Gospel Centre – newly formed group intending to become an organized church
HMB – Home Mission Board of the Southern Baptist Convention (now NAMB)
Houseboat – boat with superstructure resembling a small house
IMB – International Mission Board (formerly FMB)

JB - Johor Bahru (a city at the southern tip of the Malay Peninsula)

Jesselton – capital city of Sabah, Malaysia (now Kota Kinabalu)

KB – Kuala Belait – small town in Brunei Darussalam; near Seria

KK - Kota Kinabalu (capital city of Sabah, Malaysia - formerly Jesselton)

KL – Kuala Lumpur (capital city of Malaysia)

Kuching – capital city of Sarawak, Malaysia

Kwangsi – province in south central China (now Gwangxi)

Kweilin – city in the south central Chinese province of Kwangsi (now Guilin)

Longhouse – multiple homes under one long roof with common veranda

Malay – official language of Malaysia; also called Bahasa Malaysia (BM)

Malaya – Malay Peninsula; formerly a British colony; now part of Malaysia

Malays – indigenous peoples of the Malay Peninsula

Mandarin – most widely spoken language of China

Maoris – Polynesian people native to New Zealand

MBC – Malaysia Baptist Convention

Miri – city on northwest coast of Sarawak, Malaysia

MK – Missionary Kid (children of missionaries)

Mt. Kinabalu – tallest mountain in Southeast Asia (13,455 feet) in northwest Sabah

Ningpo (Ningbo) – city on east coast of China, near Shanghai

Penang – island off the northwest coast of Malaya and name of a Malaysian state

Primary School – elementary school; grades 1-6

Queue – long, pigtail worn by Chinese men in the 19th century

Rodheim – small German town near Frankfurt am Main

Sabah – an East Malaysian state on the island of Borneo (formerly North Borneo)

Sandakan – a city on the northeast coast of Sabah, Malaysia

Sarawak – an East Malaysian state on the southwestern side of Borneo

SAS – Singapore American School

SBC – Southern Baptist Convention

Secondary School – junior and high school; grades 7-11 (Form 1-5)

Seria – oil-rich town in Brunei Darussalam

Singapore – an island at the southern tip of the Malay Peninsula

SLCC – Successful Living Correspondence Course

Straits Settlements – former British colony in Southeast Asia, including Penang Island

TEE – Theological Education by Extension

Terrace Houses – a long row of attached houses, one or more stories high

The Bund – the quay along the waterfront in Shanghai

Training Union – small group meetings in Baptist churches to train church members

UEP – Urban Evangelism Program

Victrola – a wind-up machine which played records

WMU – Woman's Missionary Union (organization in Southern Baptist churches)

Zero – Japanese fighter plane during World War II

PROLOGUE

The piercing wail of the siren woke me from a deep sleep. Immediately my dad was by my bedside telling me to dress quickly and grab a jacket. It would be cool in the cave. This was no new event in my six-year-old life, so it was easy to go through the motions of getting dressed while still half-asleep. In no time, our family of five was trooping out of the house, out of the mission compound, out of the city's gates and towards the mountains that dotted the surrounding area.

The year was 1943 and World War II was well under way in China, where we lived. As we trudged across the bridge spanning the moat surrounding the city of Kweilin, in Kwangsi province, I wondered how long we would spend in the caves today, and whether our house would be standing when we returned. Within thirty minutes, we had reached a nearby mountain. Hordes of town folks filled the same path we had taken but most of them stopped in the lower, larger cave. Our family climbed higher up the mountain to a smaller cave, hoping to avoid being crammed into close quarters with many who might have tuberculosis or other contagious diseases. Just as we walked inside the cave we heard the Japanese bombers arriving overhead. Quickly we moved to the deepest recesses of the darkness knowing that the farther we were from the mouth of the cave the safer we would be from the falling bombs and subsequent shrapnel flying through the air outside.

My father lit some candles and my mother opened her basket. This was a large, wicker basket that she kept packed and ready to go at a moment's notice. It contained non-perishable food, such as cookies and peanuts, and water to drink. The basket also contained books. Because we never knew how long these air raids would last, Mother had no intention of us wasting time. School lessons could still be taught in a cave, while bombs fell on our city below!

Another missionary family arrived at this moment, and I was glad to see my best friends Carolyn and Ralph. It was always more fun when their family came to hide in the same cave with us. No one wanted to sleep again now, so my friends' father offered to read to us. We all sat entranced as he read from <u>The House at Pooh Corner</u>, by A.A. Milne. This was my first introduction to that loveable bear and his friends, long before Walt Disney made them famous.

We children dozed off after several enjoyable chapters although our parents, no doubt, stayed awake listening to the sounds of bombs exploding in the city below. This air raid only lasted a few hours. The "all clear" siren that told us the Japanese planes were gone awakened us - it was safe to come out of our hiding places and go home. I can still see my brothers, George and Howard, standing beside me at the mouth of the cave looking down over the city of Kweilin. Together we counted the fires burning, caused by the night's bombing raid. Many houses were destroyed or damaged that day. We tried to guess if one of those fires was our house. Praise God! In the almost seven years that we lived under these daily attacks, our house was always spared.

The First Seven Years

1937-1943

My life on this earth began at 5:25 p.m. on Sunday afternoon, April 11, 1937. Two older brothers, George Robert and Howard Thomas, had to extend their afternoon nap that day until after I arrived - an imposition for which they have never forgiven me. My parents' first child, Carolyn Ruth, died at birth so, after two sons, the birth of a healthy baby girl brought much celebration. My father named me Dorothy Lord Bausum, but it was many years before I came to understand, and appreciate, the significance of his choice.

It would seem that they spoiled me from the beginning, causing my older brothers much consternation. When I was three months old Japan invaded Manchuria and, thereafter, George and Howard took great pleasure in blaming my birth for causing World War II. In later years they even formed an R.A.D. Club which stood for "**R**ebellion **A**gainst **D**orothy." They were the only two members until my father made them let me join, whereupon they renamed it the Good Times Convention. All in all they were good big brothers, though, and we spent many happy hours playing together on the mission compound where we lived.

I was four years old when it became apparent that I needed my tonsils removed. Competent doctors were in short supply and there was no surgeon at our Baptist Hospital. One day when I was very sick there came a knock on our door. There stood a total stranger, asking for a place to spend the night. He explained that he was a German Jew, a refugee from the Nazi threats in his home country. My mother was normally very hospitable, but her heart sank at this imposition when I was so sick. Nevertheless, she welcomed the stranger, made a bed for him and set another plate at the dinner table.

During dinner my parents learned that this refugee was an ear, nose and throat specialist. The only thing he was able to escape Germany with was a small bag that contained his surgical instruments. He was concerned at my illness and offered to remove my tonsils as a way to return some of my parents' kindnesses to him. There in our Baptist Hospital this refugee specialist surgeon brought relief to my previously ill body. Whenever my mother told this story she would always quote the Bible verse from Hebrews 13:2, "Do not forget to entertain strangers, for by so doing some people have entertained angels without knowing it."

When each of us reached school age our mother taught us, with the help of the Calvert School Correspondence Course out of Baltimore, Maryland. Our education was in good hands since she was a trained schoolteacher. We grew up speaking Chinese, of course, since that was the only language we heard outside of our home. However, Mother was so determined for us to learn proper English that she required us to speak that language when we entered our house. Thus, we learned fluent Chinese from our playmates and fluent English from our parents - the best way for children to learn languages.

We attended the Kweilin Baptist Church where my father was pastor. Memories formed in that old stone building came flooding back when I revisited it in 1991. However, the clearest memory I have is of Sunday, April 12, 1942, when my two brothers were baptized. At only five years of age I did not really understand the commitment they had made, but I knew they loved God and that I would follow them in that path as soon as my dad would allow it.

The last one and a half years we were in China we had two other American missionary children to play with, Carolyn and Ralph Cauthen, children of a new missionary couple - Baker James and Eloise Cauthen. This gave a new dimension to our everyday life. For the most part, however, my memories from those first seven years of my life were centered on war events and the almost daily air raids upon our city. The wail of the siren, which blew to warn us of approaching enemy planes, became so embedded in my mind that a noontime siren blown at a factory in my college town, ten years later, still caused me to jump as though preparing to run.

****

Our family had been away from home for some much needed rest and was on a houseboat traveling up the Li River, returning to Kweilin. The boat was small, our quarters crowded, and the trip would take at least eight days. We needed to be entertained!

"Tell us a story, Daddy!" we three children pleaded.

"OK," he answered with a sly grin. "I will tell you how my mother's father married my father's mother."

He had our attention!

THE STORY

More than one hundred years ago, in Germany, there lived a man named John George Bausum. His family had been farmers for generations, living in the little town of Rodheim. John George, however, felt another calling. As a young man he left his parents and brother, and the only home he had ever known, to travel to England. There he studied the Bible and became consumed with the Great Commission that Jesus gave just before He returned to heaven. With his worldview widened, John George boarded a ship and headed for Southeast Asia. His main place of ministry was in Malaya where he worked among the Chinese and Malays on the Malayan Peninsula.

Because he had gone to Asia without financial support from any mission agency, John George soon invested in some property. It contained nutmeg and various fruit trees that produced crops he could sell to support himself and the work to which God had called him.

John George served faithfully for eight years as a bachelor missionary, although he, no doubt, hoped to have a family of his own some day. Where would he find a wife so far from his homeland?

There were missionaries from various denominations serving on the island of Penang. One family he became well acquainted with was named Dyer. They were from England and had been in Asia for many years, serving with the London Missionary Society. The husband, Samuel, was very involved in mission work around Asia and traveled quite often. His wife, Maria, had been instrumental in starting schools to educate girls, because Asian girls were often kept at home rather than allowed to attend school. The Dyers had three small children - Samuel, Burella, and Maria. The whole family prayed and talked about going to China as missionaries when that country would allow foreigners to enter. A special bond seemed to form between this family and the lonely bachelor from Germany.

One day John George heard the sad news that Samuel Dyer had passed away while on a trip to Hong Kong. Maria had recently sent her son, Samuel, to England to study. Even though her husband had died, Maria was committed to stay in Penang where she could continue the girls' school that she had begun. Her two daughters, Burella and Maria, were still with her.

John George was overwhelmed with sorrow for the widow Dyer trying to raise her small children alone in a foreign land, so he proposed marriage to her. Although she was older than him by several years, Maria realized that he would be a good companion for her in serving the Lord. Her children needed a father, also, so she accepted his proposal. They were married and settled down to ministry on Penang Island, while John George also continued his ministry in Province Wellesley on the mainland of Malaya. Later that *year he purchased a large family Bible and wrote his name and the year, 1845, on the inside front page.*

The next two years were a happy time for the four of them. John George had been without a family and found pure joy in the companionship of wife and children. As for the Dyers, they took great comfort in having a husband and father again. Life in the home was good and God was blessing their schools and church. Then tragedy struck. Maria became ill and died. John George was heartbroken. She had been his first love and a dear companion in the Lord. With a heavy heart he buried her in the London Missionary Society vault in the nearby Christian cemetery in Penang. Carefully he placed in his family Bible a delicate, filigreed design of an "M" taken from her funeral flowers. Then he turned to the more practical aspect of caring for Maria's children.

Because they were British, and Maria had family in England, John George corresponded with her brother and they decided the girls should return to their homeland to complete their education along with their brother, Samuel. With a heavy heart, John George placed them on a ship in the company of other missionaries returning home. Once again lonely, now a widower, his days were consumed with the ministry to which God had called him.

****

"Come, children! Watch how the coolies are pulling the houseboat up the river." At my dad's calling, we quickly ran out on the deck.

"Why are they pulling the boat?" I asked

"The river water is too shallow here, and we are going upstream," he explained. "The men have attached those heavy ropes to the boat there, see? Now look how they have made a loop at the other end to go around their shoulders. As they walk along the shore they pull and the boat goes forward."

"Why are they making that weird sound?" Howard wondered.

"They are chanting together so they will pull together," George explained importantly.

When we reached one of the 365 rapids on our journey the coolies came back on board the boat and switched to using bamboo poles in order to have better control as we passed through dangerous, rushing waters. Each man put the padded end of a pole against his shoulder, stuck the sharp end into the riverbed and pushed. This was done in rhythm, also, with the men walking in tandem from the bow to the stern.

We stood watching the drama for a long time. The men had to work hard to keep the boat moving along safely, but we were enjoying the ride! Finally we got bored. There was so little to do on this small houseboat.

"Hey, Dad!" George exclaimed. "You told us about John George and Maria, but you didn't explain about how your father's mother married your mother's father."

"Well, maybe there's time for the next installment before Mom has supper ready," Dad grinned.

THE STORY

John George was lonely after Maria died and he missed the children as they were away in England. Of course they wrote letters, but it wasn't the same. He did not have a family to share with him in the daily ministry. In the course of time, he met other missionaries and one day he met a British lady named Jemima Poppy. She had been in Borneo since 1844, working alongside a missionary couple in sharing the Gospel with the Dyak people. When the missionary wife died, it was necessary for Jemima to go elsewhere and the Lord led her to Penang. John George knew she was a hard worker for the Lord and, after praying about the matter, God led him to propose marriage to Miss Poppy. She accepted and they were married in Singapore in St. Andrew's Cathedral. It was a requirement for British subjects living in British colonies to be married in the Church of England. The next day they sailed to Penang.

Once again John George had someone to share his home and work. How grateful he was not to be alone! Soon a beautiful baby girl was born and they named her Mary Elizabeth. In time God blessed their home with a son, George Frederick. The boy was named after John George's only brother whom he had not seen since leaving Germany many years before. Next was William Henry, the third child, followed by two more children - Samuel Gottlieb and Louisa Jane. After six years of enjoying a growing, happy family, tragedy struck again in quick succession. In 1854 little Samuel died of smallpox and eleven months later Louisa Jane died of "the 9 days disease." They buried the little ones in the same vault with Maria.

Their home was still filled with joy. The work was growing and pleasing to God. The fruit trees were producing and supporting their needs. It would seem that all was well. However, like most missionaries of that era and place, their eyes were turned towards the great land of China. Previously that country would not allow foreigners to enter, but things were changing. Doors were opening, and John George and Jemima also talked and prayed about maybe moving on to a new field. However, there was the ministry they had begun in Malaya which needed to be continued. They corresponded with other mission groups hoping to find one who would want to take it over, but nothing seemed to be opening up at this time.

Jemima was busy with the three children, the home, and teaching at the school. John George, worn down by church

*responsibilities, came home one morning in August 1855
after having been up all night with a dying church member.
He was exhausted and collapsed on Jemima's shoulder. The
tropical heat was oppressive but even though she fanned
him, he did not revive. Then his breathing became heavy
and irregular. After several hours of excruciating pain, he
breathed his last and went to his eternal reward. Jemima
took her pen and with a heavy heart wrote the details in
the family Bible. The church members helped her lay John
George Bausum to rest in the same vault where Maria Dyer
and the Bausum infants were buried. Now Jemima was a
widow with three small children, living in a foreign land.*

****

It was great to finally reach Kweilin and get off that tiny
houseboat. Once again we had room to run about and play.
Life was back to "normal" with our daily school lessons
and, of course, the constant air raids. My dad was extremely
busy with the church as well as various Mission responsibilities. Besides these, the war took a great toll on him as a
continual flow of refugees passed through Kweilin, needing
assistance.

He served for a time as Contract Chaplain at the U.S.
Air Force base located just outside of Kweilin town. I have
some distinct memories of worshiping there as my dad
preached. One day we went out to the base and everyone
was excited because they had just captured a Japanese Zero
fighter plane. While we watched, one of the pilots took the
Zero up and flew it around. When he attempted to land,
however, the landing gear did not come down so those
on the ground waved him off. Because the radio was not
working, the pilot did not know what was wrong and tried
to land again. While those on the ground kept waving him
off, someone found some white adhesive tape and wrote on

the side of a P-40 plane, "wheels not down - pump." After awhile he got the landing gear unstuck and brought the Zero down, skidding to a successful landing. We all ran over to see it and I remember taking my finger and pushing on the outside of the plane. The metal went in and then popped back out, just like a cheap tin can!

One day we had an extended air raid and spent the entire day hiding in our little cave. After we had done school lessons, played games, and eaten lunch, we had run out of activities to amuse ourselves. Dad decided to pick up the family history where he had left off.

THE STORY

By this time the two Dyer girls, Burella and Maria, had finished their studies in England. Fulfilling their parents' dream, they went to China as missionaries. There in the city of Ningpo they taught in a school where Miss Mary Ann Aldersey was the headmistress. Because both girls were still young, this older single woman acted as their guardian.

When John George died in Penang, the girls wrote to Jemima inviting her to come to China to teach in the same school. Jemima saw this as God's leading. It took some time to settle the Bausum affairs in Penang as she had to sell the land with the fruit trees, as well as the school and church property and the house where they lived. She was pleased when the Burmah Road Gospel Hall bought the property and continued the ministry for the Lord that her husband had begun many years before.

Jemima took her daughter, Mary Elizabeth, to England and placed her in a boarding school to complete her education. Then she and the two boys, George Frederick and William Henry, sailed for Ningpo, China. Jemima found a closely-knit missionary community there with all the denominations fellowshipping together. Miss Aldersey was quite straight-laced and somewhat hard to work with, but Jemima was glad to be with Burella and Maria again.

After some time she decided to take her boys to England and leave them in school there. She was especially lonely returning to China with none of her family, but she threw herself into the ministry of sharing the Gospel, even as she had done while a single missionary in Borneo, before marrying John George Bausum.

One of the long-time members of this close-knit community in Ningpo was an American Baptist Union missionary, Dr. Edward Clemens Lord. His first wife and their two small children had died from illnesses some years before. Now he was married again and had five young children. Dr. Lord was a highly respected member of the missionary community and an able peacemaker when disagreements arose.

Some time after Jemima arrived in Ningpo Dr. Lord's wife took sick and died. This was a terrible blow to him, and the care of the children was time-consuming. Dr. Lord soon began to look for wife number three. He found her in Jemima and they were married in October 1861. Having lost two wives and two children, Dr. Lord decided it would be best to send his five children back to the United States, as life in China was most difficult. He had an aunt (Mrs. Esther Lord McNeill) living in New York State who was willing to care for his children, so Jemima escorted the Lord children to America. Because her own two sons were not doing well in their studies in England, she decided to bring them to America, as well. Therefore, the five Lord children and the two Bausum children went to live with Aunt Esther. Mary Elizabeth remained in England as she was happy in her school. Jemima then returned to China where she served alongside her husband, Dr. Lord, until her death. Dr. Lord lived to be seventy, and outlived three more wives after Jemima.

When the all clear siren blew that afternoon, we were almost sorry. We still had not learned what my dad meant by, "My father's mother married my mother's father!"

****

My dad became very ill with septicemia during the winter of 1942, and was not responding to any of the available medications. His condition deteriorated in January 1943 and one night it appeared that death was near. I was not yet six years old but, in my mind's eye, I can still see my dad, wrapped in comforters, shivering and huddling close to a red-hot stove. George ran across the compound to get a doctor from our Baptist Hospital. She came running and, after giving Dad a shot of adrenalin, she administered a sulfa drug that was new on the market. "We will try this," she said. Praise the Lord, it worked! The infection was almost gone within a week, but Dad needed some extended rest to recuperate completely.

We took the houseboat down to Wuchow and spent the next month with Dr. Bill Wallace, a Foreign Mission Board (FMB) missionary serving there (later martyred by the Communists in 1951). I remember him being extremely busy, seldom at home, but a very kind person. We were there when my mom celebrated her birthday and I have never forgotten how Dr. Wallace remembered that important date by asking his cook to bake a cake for her. That truly impressed this little girl! By late March, my dad was able to return to Kweilin and resume his many wartime responsibilities and our family settled back down to life at home.

As 1943 was ending, my parents realized our days in China were numbered. The Japanese were moving steadily south and would soon reach Kweilin. We did not wish to be there when they arrived! Given his connections with the American Air Force, my dad began to make plans for us to fly out of Kweilin. Since we were civilians, however, military personnel and needs took priority. We were booked to fly several times and then at the last moment the flights were cancelled.

****

Kweilin, Kwangsi, China

Vault where John George Bausum
is buried in Penang, Malaysia

Church in Ningpo, China - possibly built by Dr. E.C. Lord

Robert Bausum Family: Back row – Howard, George (about 1943) Front row – Robert, Dorothy, Euva

THE SECOND SEVEN YEARS

1944-1950

*J*have a very clear memory of January 3, 1944 when my dad announced that we were to fly in two days. We had 44 hours to close up the house, pack, say good-bye to our friends, and leave. My dad did not sleep during those days. He had many responsibilities to hand over to others, as well as all that was involved in getting us ready to leave. We carefully packed away most of our things in the attic of our house, expecting to return the next year, hoping the war would be over by then. Even today I can return to that attic, in my memory, as I tucked my doll "Peggy" into her bed, kissed her good-bye, and told her I would see her next year.

Wednesday, January 5, 1944 came and we actually got on the plane this time. Later we learned that it was the last flight which carried civilians out of Kweilin. Those who left after us had to travel by overcrowded buses or trains. Our first stop was Kunming, the capital city of Yunnan province, due west of Kwangsi province. There we waited a few days for another plane that would fly us to India.

At last, we boarded a plane that had no heat. We were wearing several layers of clothes to keep warm and as another way to carry more clothes with us. Each person could only carry thirty pounds of baggage, so wearing extra clothes made room in the suitcases for other important items.

Our plane flew over "the hump" which was the allied pilots' name for an air route by which they flew supplies from India across Burma into China to re-supply the American Flying Tigers and the Chinese army. This route took us over the eastern end of the Himalayan Mountains that separate China from India.

Because of fear of detection by enemy radar, we flew at treetop level. This meant the plane flew up and down, following the terrain of the mountains. I can personally testify that this was quite conducive to airsickness!

We finally reached Calcutta where other missionaries helped us find hotel rooms. We still had a two-day train trip ahead of us, crossing India from East to West, to reach Bombay where we planned to board a ship for America. I remember seeing wild animals roaming free as I looked out the window of that crowded train.

We had to wait in Bombay for several days for the ship that would take us to America. At last, we had time to catch our breath and Dad finally could relax a bit and pick up the story of our ancestors.

THE STORY

You will remember that there were five Lord children and two Bausum children living with Aunt Esther in New York State. They grew up in the same house like brothers and sisters but were related only through the marriage of their parents. Dr. Lord had married Mrs. Bausum and all their children were living together with his aunt. Meanwhile the parents continued to serve as missionaries in Ningpo, China.

The fourth child of Dr. Lord was Fannie Adaline. When she reached seventeen years of age and had finished her schooling, she returned to Ningpo to live with her father for a while. Besides his missionary work, Dr. Lord was serving the United States Government as a Consul in Ningpo, so Fannie worked alongside him as his secretary. She wrote all of his correspondence by hand since there were no type-writers. This fact would be most helpful to her many years later when she came to live with me in China.

Fannie returned to America after several years and married one of the Bausum boys she had grown up with at Aunt Esther's house. William Henry Bausum married Fannie Adaline Lord in Chicago on August 26, 1885. They received news on their wedding day that William's brother,

George Frederick, had died in Pierre, South Dakota the day before. Immediately, William left his new bride in Chicago and traveled to South Dakota to help in this time of tragedy. George had been a widower and left behind a son, George Adelpheus. Now William Henry took the young boy back to New York State to be raised by none other than Aunt Esther!

When William returned to Chicago and his bride, they made final preparations and headed for South Dakota to live. Taking advantage of the government's offer of 160 acres of land, they settled in "the boot" of the Missouri River and built a sod house for their first home. Later, when their land became part of an Indian reservation, they had to move farther north where they staked their claim about three and one-half miles west of Harrold, South Dakota. They built a house on the banks of Medicine Creek and that is where I was born.

"Now do you understand what I meant when I said my father's mother married my mother's father?"

We looked at Dad in bewilderment for a second.

"William was your father!" George exclaimed.

"Fannie was your mother," chimed in Howard.

"William's mother was **Jemima**" I added, "and Fannie's father was **Dr. Lord**."

"Right!" grinned my dad. "My **father's mother** married my **mother's father**."

****

The day had arrived for us to board the ship in Bombay that would take us to America. I would see my homeland for the first time in my almost-seven years of life. It was exciting, but once we got on board the ship it was disappointing. The ship was very crowded. There were Australian army personnel and New Zealand Maoris returning home from the war in Northern Africa. One thousand Italian prisoners of war were in the "brig" in the lower levels of the ship. Of course, there were various crew members and about 200 civilians like us. The ship was a luxury liner, the SS Mariposa, which the government had commandeered for use in wartime.

The few women on board were put all together on Deck C, located below the water line. There were no portholes on Deck C and it was stifling hot. The men shared cabins on Decks A & B and then soldiers were sleeping all over the decks outside because there were not enough cabins. Being a girl, I was sent to Deck C with my mother. I hated the separation from my dad and I was jealous of my brothers because they were with him. On top of that, it was so hot in the women's quarters that I became ill. I do not know how he did it, but my dad got permission for me to sleep in the cabin with him and my brothers so that I would not be sick. My poor mother had to make the whole journey sleeping in Deck C. Happily we could all be together when it was not time for sleeping.

Because it was wartime, our ship had to zigzag across the Pacific Ocean, dodging enemy submarines. In this way, it took one month and two days to reach the United States from India, instead of a normal two to three weeks. Everyone on board was required to carry a lifejacket with them at all times and we had daily lifeboat drills. All the lifejackets were adult sized and very heavy, so for me to lug one around was most difficult. Usually my dad would carry mine for me. However, if the Military Police (MP) saw you without a lifejacket they would scold you and send you to get it, so whenever we saw an MP approaching, my dad would quickly pass my life jacket to me until they had passed.

Sitting on the deck one day, surrounded by us three children, my dad continued his narration of our family history.

THE STORY

Well, you now understand why I said, "My father's mother married my mother's father." Jemima Bausum and Dr. Edward Clemens Lord were my grandparents. My father was born in Malaya and my mother was born in China because their parents were missionaries. Although my parents grew up together at Aunt Esther's home in New York State, they kept in touch with their parents overseas and knew about their mission work with the Chinese. "Missions" was always an important topic in our family. In fact, all of my growing up years we heard stories, not only about our grandparents, but about my Aunt Mary who was a missionary in China.

Mary Elizabeth Bausum was the first child of John George and Jemima Bausum. She was my father's older sister. After John George died, Jemima took her children to England and left them in a boarding school there. Later, because George and William were not doing well in school, she took them to America to grow up under the care of Aunt Esther Lord. Mary was happy in England, however, so her mother left her there. When she was seventeen years old, Mary finished her education and traveled by ship to China with Mr. and Mrs. Hudson Taylor who were also missionaries in Ningpo. Mrs. Taylor was the former Maria Dyer - Mary's stepsister. Mary went to Ningpo and lived with her mother who was married to Dr. Lord. She had felt the call to serve God in China and began working alongside her mother and stepfather.

At that time Hudson Taylor was establishing what would later become the China Inland Mission (CIM) – now the Overseas Missionary Fellowship. From time to time new recruits were coming from England to serve with him. One of these, Stephen Paul Barchet, arrived in August 1866 and met the Lords and Mary Bausum. Stephen and Mary were married in Ningpo two years later, and served together as missionaries for the rest of their lives. Like John George

Bausum, the father-in-law he never knew, Stephen was also a German who somehow found his way to England and from there to the mission field.

After serving with the CIM for several years, Stephen left their ministry and from then on related to Dr. Lord, his step-father-in-law, and the American Baptist Union's missionary work in and around Ningpo. In later years Stephen and Mary served as missionaries in Shanghai, China and that is where they died and are buried.

George looked thoughtful. "So your grandparents were missionaries, but your parents were not?"

"That is basically true," Dad answered. "However, my mother did return to the mission field two different times - once before she was married, to help her father, and once after I had become a missionary, to help me. But that story will have to wait until another day."

****

The ship made two stops, one in Australia and one in New Zealand, where soldiers and prisoners were unloaded. We also picked up some New Zealand soldiers who were en route to Canada for their final training before going into battle. For the remainder of the trip it was not so crowded. Because we had to dodge submarines, the ship crossed the international dateline twice, giving us an extra day. Since this occurred in February, and 1944 was a leap year, those of us on board had thirty days in February that year. Gratefully, the enemy submarines never found us and we reached American waters early one cold, February morning. My dad called me up on deck to see the shoreline of California. "Look Dorothy," he exclaimed. "You can see America!" I had heard so much about my homeland and had been so excited to see it that the grey, distant shoreline was disappointing to an almost-seven-year old little girl.

After one month and two days on the ocean, we docked in San Pedro early in the afternoon of February 25, 1944. The military personnel went ashore first, of course, so we civilians waited our turn. Then there was various "red tape" to go through as everyone's papers had to be checked. The officials took us alphabetically and although our name began with a "B" it was midnight before we finally got off that ship.

The ship's kitchen had shut down after breakfast so we were starving! As long as I live I shall never forget what happened next. There on the dock were long tables, loaded with sandwiches and other food. Women of the Red Cross had prepared this and then had patiently waited for us to disembark so they could welcome us back to our country. We were invited to eat all we wanted. I can still taste that first sandwich and, although I have no idea what the ingredients were, it was the most delicious thing I have ever eaten. Other women loaded us into their personal cars and drove the thirty miles to Los Angeles where they had booked hotel rooms for all these returning civilians.

My dad had to return to the ship with our driver because our trunks had not yet been unloaded, but our mom and we three kids settled into a real hotel room. After the crowded conditions on that ship it was like heaven! When I asked for a drink of water I learned, for the first time in my life, that it was OK to drink water out of the faucet without first boiling it. Taking that first drink of un-boiled water, and staring out the window at the blinking neon lights, I finally realized that America was not just a grey shoreline, but also a truly marvelous place.

Soon my dad purchased a car and we headed across country to visit my mother's family in Texas. On the way we stopped to see the Painted Desert, Grand Canyon and other sights. It was at the Grand Canyon that I saw my first snow. I was daily experiencing "firsts" in my young life!

When we reached McKinney, Texas, in late March, I met my mother's side of our family for the first time. This meant that they were also meeting me for the first time, although my brothers had been there on a previous furlough before I was born. All the aunts and uncles were trying to decide whom I looked like, and I was growing shyer by the moment. Then my precious Granny Majors spoke up in her practical, gentle way, "I think she looks like Dorothy!" She won my heart.

****

We enrolled in the McKinney public school system where I entered the first grade. I had already completed the first grade through the Calvert School studies, and my brothers had finished the fifth and sixth grades. We were just put into those same grades to help us learn what it was like to attend an American school. For me it was quite traumatic. My grades were fine, as my mother had taught me well, but learning my way around in this new culture was not so easy. We were different. We spoke another language as well as English. We didn't know the latest American slang. Truly, we needed those two months to just attend class and adjust before trying to enter a new grade in the fall.

The most important event in my life occurred while we were in McKinney. I had wanted to be baptized when I was five years old, along with my brothers, but my dad knew I did not really understand and so he wisely told me I must wait until I was seven. On Sunday, April 9, 1944, when the pastor gave the invitation to accept Jesus, I walked down the aisle of First Baptist Church, McKinney, Texas. My parents had no forewarning that I was going to make this deci-sion, but I knew what I was doing. That day I asked Jesus to save me from my sin, and I set my seven-year-old heart on making Jesus my Lord for the rest of my life. It was my spiritual birthday. I was born again! My dad baptized me in my mother's home church on April 23, 1944, an event I can still clearly picture in my mind's eye, sixty-plus years later.

Our family hit the road again when school was out for the summer. We said good-bye to Mother's family and headed for Maryland to meet Dad's family. We had one stop to make on the way, however. Returning missionaries always need to have thorough physical check-ups and, after eight years in China, my parents were certainly in need of this. We all checked into the Baptist Hospital in New Orleans, Louisiana for several days. It turned out that Mom needed surgery so we extended our stay in New Orleans by a number of weeks. We children had the privilege of attending our first English Vacation Bible School (VBS) at the Rachel Sims Mission. As we were meeting more new children this was not always a pleasant experience for three missionary kids, but I do remember learning the chorus to that joyful hymn, "Serve the Lord with Gladness" while in that VBS.

Finally, we reached Annapolis, Maryland where the entire Bausum clan was present to greet us. They were all so proud of my dad and mom that we children felt right at home. Soon our parents went house-hunting and bought a house in Baltimore. We moved in just in time to enroll in the Baltimore public school system in September 1944.

****

I entered the second grade, Howard the sixth, and George the seventh. Howard and I attended the same school, Public School # 236, for that first year which was a great help to me. We walked to and from school together. Sometimes other kids teased us, perhaps because we did not talk or act just like other American kids. I do not remember any details - only that Howard was by my side and gave me courage. As winter approached, we had a heavy snowfall and they cancelled school. We three "China Kids" played outside until we were practically frozen and could barely put one foot in front of the other. What a thrilling and exhilarating experience! When we finally had to come inside the house to thaw out we discovered that "snow days" could be long and boring.

"Can you tell us some more stories about our family, Dad?" I asked.

Ever ready to entertain, as well as educate us, he was quick to respond.

THE STORY

*Well, let us see. I have told you about John George and Jemima, about Dr. Lord and his five children, and about Mary Elizabeth and Paul. That brings us to **my** generation. My parents, William Henry and Fannie Adaline, had settled in South Dakota. My sister Jennie June was their first child, born on June 24, 1886. Three sons followed in close order: John Edward on May 13, 1888, Frederic William on October 12, 1889, and Benjamin Franklin on February 13, 1892. I was the fourth boy, and came into this world on a blustery March 22, 1893. There were two more boys born after me: Thomas Howard born on April 25, 1896, and Charles Henry born on October 11, 1897. Unfortunately, these two boys died at an early age, which left me the youngest in the family.*

Life on the prairie was hard and the older boys had to work alongside my father in running the ranch, where we raised sheep, horses, and cows. Jennie, of course, became my mother's right hand helper, but I managed to escape a lot of the hard work as the youngest. I had chores, of course, but I was always privileged to attend school, as was my brother Ben. My two older brothers, however, had to drop out of school after a few years because they had to help work the ranch.

When I was twelve years old, my parents decided it just was not worth it to continue working so hard with so little to show for it, while depriving their children of a proper education. Therefore, they made the decision to move to Annapolis, Maryland where the son of Paul and Mary Barchet had bought property. It was their plan to live with the Barchets until they were able to buy and establish their own farm.

Moving was quite a chore as we not only packed up clothes and furniture but also moved horses and milk cows. John and Ben left first and traveled by train with one carload of furniture and some horses. My mother, Jennie, and I left second, by passenger train, and traveled to New York for a visit with Aunt Esther Lord and other family members. Father and Fred came three months later, after selling the ranch and stock as well as settling any accounts. They traveled with a car load of milk cows. The move was well-planned and carried out except for one unforeseen event, which forever changed our lives.

The train Father and Fred were traveling on stopped in Cumberland, Maryland and Father went to buy some food for them to eat. Their train began to move as he was returning across the railroad tracks and he ran to catch it. Suddenly, another train sped around a curve, hit and killed Father. Fred was waiting for him and saw it happen. He jumped off the train and stayed with Father's body until he was able to arrange to move his body on to Annapolis where we buried him. As we all were reunited in Annapolis, the move completed, we were missing the head of our family, our strong and loving father, Mother's husband.

Fortunately, John and Fred were old enough to run the farm we eventually bought, while Ben and I were able to attend school and complete our high school education. Jennie continued as Mother's right hand helper in the home. It was a hard struggle for us all, but Mother was a woman of *strong faith, and the Lord brought us through.*

We three were subdued as Dad finished this part of the story. He had work to do, so the rest would wait for another day, but we each moved off to our own activities grateful that we still had the head of our family, our dad.

****

Life in Baltimore, Maryland became more and more busy and story-telling time less and less available. My dad often was gone from home, speaking in Schools of Missions. These were one-or two-week-long meetings sponsored by Baptist Associations, where the missionaries spoke in a different church each night. Mother did not get to go to as many of these meetings because we three children were still at home. Our education continued in the public school system of Baltimore and, because we were delayed in returning to China, eventually George and Howard graduated from high school there and went on to college.

The first few years that we lived in Baltimore we joined the Gregory Memorial Baptist Church (GMBC) which was pastored by W.H. Brannock, my dad's friend from college and seminary days. He asked Mom and Dad to begin a Junior Church that would provide a worship time for children under the age of thirteen while their parents were attending the regular worship service. This was a great success in many ways. Dad appointed Howard and another boy as the "pastors" which meant they took turns presiding during the service. My dad preached the sermon. A choir was organized and we presented special music regularly. When I was about ten years old, another girl and I began taking turns being the pianist for the services. We were involved in this ministry for about two years and many children accepted Jesus as their Savior. The work continued for many years after our family left. This experience was a defining point in my personal spiritual growth as I began to learn to use the gifts God had given me for His service.

My dad was Camp Missionary for a Children's camp the summer after I turned ten. George, Howard, and I went along as campers. One scene from that camp remains as clear in my mind today as it was that night at camp. It was the last night and we were all gathered around a big campfire. We sang songs of praise and worship and my dad brought a message of challenge, to accept Christ as Savior and to follow Him in full-time Christian service. Those responding to God's call stepped forward and stood closer to the campfire. God spoke clearly to me that night that He wanted me to be a foreign missionary when I grew up. I stepped forward and immediately felt an arm go around my waist. George was already standing there, giving his life for fulltime service wherever God would lead. This call from God, reaffirmed from time to time, became the guiding force in my life.

My dad began to serve as Acting Pastor for two small churches in another part of Baltimore in September 1948. Our time at GMBC ended. George and Howard continued to worship there as they were teenagers by then, able to go and come on their own. I went with my parents and became involved at the Woolford Memorial and Watersedge Baptist churches. Although Woolford Memorial had a regular pianist she often could not attend, or preferred not to play, so I became the "almost" regular pianist. I specifically remember Wednesday night prayer meetings because she rarely came then.

My dad loved to choose hymns on Wednesday night that even he did not know so we could all learn them together. This habit of his taught me to be ready to play any hymn in the hymnbook. It became my habit whenever getting a new hymnbook to play through the entire book so I would never be called on to play a hymn I did not know! It was also during a Vacation Bible School at this church that I was first asked to tell a story to the other children. I was twelve years old and scared to death, but in doing this I discovered another gift that God had given me which has been my joy to use for Him ever since.

The times for sitting around as a family, listening to Dad's stories, seemed to exist no longer. However, I loved going places with my dad and one day as we were riding to an associational meeting, he continued his storytelling to me.

THE STORY

I did not know what God wanted me to do with my life after high school so I went to work in Baltimore. About two years later our sister, Jennie, became ill and passed away. It was a sobering experience that caused me to think more deeply about God's will for my life. I had known about my family background of missionaries, and had grown up in a deeply spiritual family, but I never considered myself worthy to follow such a calling. One Sunday evening after the service our pastor at College Avenue Baptist Church in Annapolis put his hand on my shoulder and asked, "Robert, have you ever thought of becoming a preacher?" Things moved swiftly after that and the pastor helped me to get a scholarship so that I could continue my education. College Avenue Baptist Church licensed me to preach and sent me off to Richmond College in the fall of 1913.

Dr. Brannock, whom you know from Gregory Memorial, became one of my best friends in college. He attended a missions conference and came back fired up about the need for missionaries to go overseas. It was only a matter of time until my call from God became a call to missions. I got permission to follow my friends on to Crozer Seminary in Chester,

Pennsylvania, without actually receiving a college degree. This school was only one hundred miles from Annapolis and there were good possibilities that I could pastor a church nearby. My friend, Brannock, recommended me for pastor at the Pimlico Mission of the First Baptist Church in Baltimore during my second year at seminary. Later they organized into the Pimlico Baptist Church and ordained me as their first pastor. I stayed there until I resigned to seek appointment under the Southern Baptist Foreign Mission Board (FMB).

During my interview for appointment, they asked me which country I wanted to serve in and my reply was, "China. That was where my ancestors were missionaries."

****

I came home from school one day with time on my hands. My dad was working on his stamp collection so I went to observe his handiwork.

"You sure have a lot of stamps from China," I noted. "Hey, that reminds me you never finished telling about what happened when you first went to China as a missionary."

That was all the prompting my dad needed!

THE STORY

Once the FMB appointed me, things moved along quickly. There was an urgent call for more missionaries to serve in Kweilin, China so that is where I was asked to go. By August 1920, I was packed and ready. It was difficult to tell my family good-bye but I had a strong sense of God's leading and was excited for what He had in store for me.

My family took me to the train station in Annapolis and I headed for Baltimore where a number of my friends from the Pimlico Baptist Church came to see me off as I boarded the train for Chicago. A representative of the FMB met me in Chicago and I joined a group of other missionaries headed for Asia. We continued traveling by train across the USA up through the Dakotas and then into Canada. At the border I had my first experience with customs formalities, which are an ongoing part of a missionary's life. Our train went through the Canadian Rockies and on to the coastal city of Vancouver where we boarded the Empress of Japan, the ship which would carry us across the Pacific Ocean.

We passed the Aleutian Islands following the Great Circle and sailed on to our first stop, Japan. From there the ship sailed to Shanghai, China, where we landed just ahead of a typhoon. I visited Aunt Mary, my father's older sister, while the ship was in port.

After a few days we sailed down the coast of China to Hong Kong where a senior missionary, Dr. C.J. Lowe, met us. We did some shopping and then headed up the river to Wuchow where we caught a houseboat that would take us to Kweilin. You remember the houseboat from Kweilin, right?

"I sure do!" I exclaimed.

That was the first time I rode one and it was a fascinating experience for me. Of course, arriving in Kweilin was even more memorable as this would be my place of service until the Lord led me elsewhere.

Language study was my first priority. I hired a tutor and set about the long process of learning Chinese - a language with different musical tones. After only three months of study I was informed that as of January 1, 1921, I would become principal of the Chu Chai Boys' School. There was no one else to take the responsibility so I found myself working in an environment where I could not even communicate with the teachers or students. It was quite a challenge!

One of the first things I did after becoming principal was to build a proper school building - quite an education in itself. I also continued my language study as well as doing some teaching in English at the school. I organized one of the first troops of Boy Scouts in China after being in Kweilin about a year and had many interesting adventures with them.

When I went to China without a wife, I assumed that it was God's will for me to remain unmarried like the apostle Paul. I envisioned myself traveling around the countryside preaching and establishing churches. Therefore, within about a year of arriving in Kweilin I made my first trip into the country. Many other trips were made in the ensuing years, each with its own excitement, danger, and testimony to God's goodness and protection. We preached the Gospel and gave out tracts to thousands of people, "sowing China down with Christian literature."

After I had been in China about one year my mother, Fannie Lord Bausum, came to live with me. When she applied for a passport to join me in China, she needed to produce a birth certificate to prove her identity. They did not want to issue her a passport because she had no birth certificate. However, you will remember when she was seventeen years old my mother returned to China to live with her father, Dr. Lord, and served as secretary for his work as the American Consul in Ningpo. All of his correspondence with the state department was written in my mother's handwriting, so when this was discovered it did not take long for the authorities to realize she really was who she said she was, and her passport was immediately forthcoming.

My mother taught school for the missionary children on our compound and kept house for me. It was wonderful having her with me and she enjoyed getting back to the land of her birth. During her time in Kweilin she was able to make several visits to her sister-in-law, Mary Elizabeth Bausum Barchet, who still lived in Shanghai.

William Henry Bausum

Fannie Adaline Lord

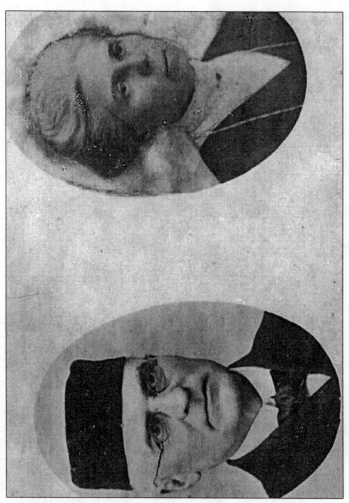

Stephen Barchet and Mary Elizabeth Bausum Barchet

William Henry Bausum Family – 1905
Back row: John, Fred, Ben;
Front row: Fannie, Robert, Jennie

Ningpo, China cemetery –1923: Freelove Lyon's grave, Robert Bausum Flora Lightfoot's grave, Fannie Lord Bausum, Edward Clemens Lord's grave

John, Fred, Robert, and Ben Bausum - 1960

Celia Rose Majors – "Granny Majors"

THE THIRD SEVEN YEARS

1951-1957

*W*e had left China in 1944 thinking we would return the next year but God has His own plans. My parents were in poor health when we first reached the USA so they needed a longer furlough for refreshing. By the time they were physically ready to return to China World War II had ended and the Communists were taking over China. I remember several times we put our house in Baltimore up for sale and began to pack for returning, only to receive a call from the Foreign Mission Board (FMB) saying the Communists had just taken over the city to which we were scheduled to go.

When it became evident that sending missionaries to mainland China was not safe, the FMB began sending China missionaries to the surrounding island countries. My parents had a choice of several places and, in the summer of 1951, they chose Taiwan. George had already finished two years at Mars Hill Baptist College and was transferring to Carson-Newman College (CNC). Howard had just graduated from high school and planned to attend CNC also. My parents and I packed for the move to Taiwan. To be quite honest, I was very angry about this move.

Having spent the past seven years in the USA, and having reached the ripe age of fourteen, the thought of a "foreign" country was not appealing to me. Furthermore, I had forgotten all the Chinese language that I spoke as a child. If there had been a better option I would not have gone with my parents. We left for Taiwan with me carrying a grudge and determined to return to the USA as soon as possible. I could complete my schoolwork as fast as I wished since I would be doing my high school studies by correspondence course. I planned to finish four years of high school in three years.

Before we left the USA my dad conducted the wedding ceremony for George and his bride, Effie Ballard, whom he had met at Mars Hill. We took Howard to CNC and then picked up Carol Lawton, a missionary kid (MK) who was going to travel with us to join her parents in Thailand. Carol was my age so the trip would be a little less stressful having another teenager along than it might have been otherwise.

We drove to San Francisco where we sold our car, bought a pickup truck for use in Taiwan, and then boarded the SS President Cleveland for Hong Kong. The voyage was pleasant overall. After a few days in Hong Kong buying various supplies, we caught a smaller ship that took us to Taiwan. The water was very choppy and we spent most of those two days in bed to avoid being thrown down on the floor whenever we tried walking around. As we stepped onto the dock in Keelung, Taiwan it seemed we did not have our balance yet, as everything was still moving. Later we learned that what we had felt was actually an earthquake welcoming us to our new home!

Life in Taiwan was very boring those first weeks so I was glad when, one day, my mother said, "Come, Dorothy. Sit beside me and let me tell you MY story. It will help us pass the time while we wait for our freight to arrive from the USA."

THE STORY

You know my mother, your Granny Majors. I regret that you never met my father as he died while we were still living in China. He was a common farmer, quiet and solid. He and my mother had seven children. I was the second child, but the first daughter. You met them all when we were living in Texas: Noah, me, Grace, Minnie, Blythe, Sam, and the baby, Ethel. She was only twelve years old when I went to China!

Granddaddy Majors was not a Christian when I was growing up, but the rest of us went to church. Later he did accept Christ. It was there I heard the Gospel and accepted Jesus as my Savior and Lord. From that moment I knew that

God had a special plan for my life even though I did not know what it was.

My father grew cotton and all of us had to work hard in the fields picking cotton. I was a bit of a dreamer in my youth and the job of picking cotton was easier for me because of this. I knew God's Word referred to the world as a "field" and the work of sharing the Gospel and bringing people to Jesus as the "harvest." Therefore, as I looked down the long rows of cotton I would imagine they were people needing Jesus. As I picked I preached to them. It helped me not to feel the pain in my back and it deepened the calling that I was feeling from God – to go and preach to the people of the world.

In the fall when the pumpkins were ripe, I would line them up in the barn and preach to them. I knew that God wanted me to share His love with the "yellow people." I cannot place a date on my call to missions. I only know that it was real and strong.

There was a flu epidemic during my final year of high school and they closed the school. Because I was always a good student with excellent grades, they let me take the teacher's examination, and I passed. I taught in a grade school that year before going on to college. By working, and with help from the Woman's Missionary Union (WMU) in my church, I graduated from Mary Hardin Baylor College in 1923.

I went to Southwestern Baptist Seminary in Fort Worth, Texas that summer and then the next full year. By 1924 the Foreign Mission Board (FMB) considered me prepared and appointed me as a missionary to China. The WMU women helped me buy what I needed and I packed my trunk. First Baptist Church in McKinney, Texas, where you were baptized, pledged to pay my salary because the FMB was short of funds, although they were able to pay my travel expenses. Off I went to China - a dream come true.

I traveled with an older single missionary, Hattie Stallings. We rode the train to San Francisco, the SS President Polk to

Hong Kong, and a houseboat, like the ones you remember, took me on to Kweilin. Among the missionaries who met me upon my arrival was a young bachelor named Robert Bausum and his mother, Mrs. Fannie Bausum.

****

Actually those first weeks in Taiwan were not boring, just frustrating. It was an exciting time in the missionary work. Four months before our arrival a single missionary named Addie Cox had come to Keelung to tell people about Jesus. When we arrived they were just waiting for a pastor to come and baptize those who had accepted Christ, and to help them establish a church. My dad was to be that pastor.

Our ship arrived in Keelung on Monday, October 22, 1951, and my dad went right to work interviewing those who had expressed a desire to follow Christ. There were nearly one hundred potential believers and, after stringent interviews, the leaders decided that fifty-seven really understood what they were doing and were ready for baptism. The others would continue to study and learn for a while longer.

Sunday, October 28, 1951, is a day that etched itself in my memory in spite of my hard, angry heart at being 'dragged off' to this foreign land. The Lord had miraculously provided the ideal place for a baptismal service. It was a Japanese-style community bath located in a military hospital. The bath was about eight by ten feet in size with walls three feet high - like a mini-swimming pool. Around the inside of this bath was a low ledge, meant for the bathers to sit on, which served as the perfect step down into the water for the new believers. There was plenty of space in the room, which we curtained off on either side to provide changing areas.

I saw my dad baptize those fifty-seven people and was overwhelmed with the wonder that they had actually cast aside their idols and wanted to follow the living Christ.

We sang the chorus of the hymn, "O Happy Day," as each believer came up out of the water. Fifty-seven-times we sang that chorus! It became a truly happy day, even for me. Back at the rented church house these fifty-seven, with their hair still wet, joined with fifteen others of us, previously baptized believers, to officially organize the Keelung Baptist Church.

"The joy I feel today reminds me of how I felt when I first arrived in Kweilin, China," my mom said as we drove the twenty miles back to the capital city of Taipei, where we were living temporarily.

"Tell me about it," I pleaded.

THE STORY

Several things impressed me deeply when I arrived in Kweilin and began to look around and meet the people. One was how many people there were filling the streets, the shops, even the church. I began to comprehend what Jesus must have felt when he saw the "multitudes." These were people living in the darkness of sin and I had the wonderful privilege to bring the Light of the World into their lives. Almost every Sunday there was a baptism service in the Kweilin Baptist Church and it was a great time of rejoicing - like what we experienced today. I just knew that God had brought me to the place where He meant for me to be - the place I had been dreaming of while picking cotton and preaching to pumpkins back in Texas.

My first, and greatest, responsibility was to learn to speak the Chinese language. Very few people spoke any English in Kweilin besides the missionaries. Learning Chinese was quite a challenge because it is so different from English, but I was determined to learn it well. Of course I made many mistakes, but the Chinese are very forgiving people in that respect because they are so pleased to see a foreigner trying to learn their language. One of the most interesting and best ways in which I felt comfortable speaking Chinese was when I talked with the little children. For one thing, they spoke the words and tones very clearly, their vocabulary was simple, and that was where I needed to begin. In addition, the children would laugh with me (not at me!) when I said something wrong, and then they would correct my mistakes.

My second responsibility was to the Pei Tseng Baptist Girls' School that was located on our compound. I began teaching in English almost immediately and took up the responsibilities of school principal long before I was fluent in Chinese. It was a most satisfying experience for me to relate to all those precious girls, helping them get a good education as well as sharing the Gospel to others in every way possible. My heart leaped for joy each time one of "my girls" asked Jesus into her heart.

The missionaries had many opportunities to see each other coming and going to our work since we all lived on the same compound. The only single male missionary, Robert Bausum, was principal of the Baptist Boys' School so he and I were often together sharing ideas, plans, and programs including both the schools. In fact, when he was on furlough from 1926-1928, I was in charge of the finances for the Boys' School so we even kept in touch by mail during that time.

People began to pair me up with this eligible bachelor soon after my arrival in Kweilin. It seemed that we were always seated next to each other whenever we attended a dinner. We single ladies invited him and his mother over to our house for meals and sometimes I was invited to their house for dinner. He had a lovely Victrola and the prettiest records that I enjoyed listening to while there. Although both of us had gone to China assuming we would remain single, God had other plans. When Robert returned from his first furlough after his mother had passed away, our relation-

ship moved to another level and we soon were engaged to be married. It may seem strange to you but this presented quite a problem for the other missionaries and, therefore, for us!

All too soon, we arrived back in Taipei where we were staying with another missionary family, the Quicks. It had been a wonderful, but tiring, day.

****

After staying for a few weeks in the missionary home of Oz and Mary Quick in Taipei, we finally moved to a rented house in Keelung where my parents were assigned to help develop the newly organized Keelung Baptist Church. The house we rented was actually the top floor of the landlord's house with him living downstairs. Although we had our own outside entrance he could actually walk up an inside stairway from his house and be in ours! Usually, he would call out our names as he approached in this manner but the situation was not ideal. Our only toilet was located halfway down those same stairs on the landing with only a few more stairs and a door separating us from the landlord's living quarters. The bathroom where we bathed and brushed our teeth was a lean-to attached to the backside of our part of the house.

This house was located on a rather high hill with the only access a steep pathway. This meant we had to park our pickup truck in the street below and walk up no matter how tired we were or what the weather might be. Since Keelung is the second rainiest spot on earth we often made that trek under an umbrella splashing mud on our feet and legs as we went. I remember so clearly the day we moved our freight from America up that steep hill. My dad hired coolies to carry everything, but the most challenging item was my old upright piano. Eight men took bamboo poles and tied them on either side of the piano. Then they tied cross poles which protruded like handles on both sides. Each man put his shoulder under one of those cross poles. The leader gave the count and on "three" they all lifted. The piano cleared the ground, they made sure of the balance, and then the long climb up that slippery hill began.

I was in our living room looking out the window as those eight men slowly and carefully made their way up to our house, the piano swinging back and forth between them. Sometimes I looked away in fear but then my curiosity demanded I watch this amazing feat. They finally made it to the door, removed the bamboo poles, and brought my piano into our living room. Gratefully, I have no memory of watching them carry it back down that hill when we moved into a permanent mission house.

My parents had promised that I could have a dog when we settled down in Keelung so very soon after moving into the rented house a friend gave me a puppy. He was a mutt, I suppose, but to me he was very special and I named him "Prince Gilbert." He was rusty in color, adorable in nature, and quickly became known as "Little Gil."

Life settled down to schoolwork, playing with Little Gil, practicing the piano, and attending church services each night. Since I had forgotten the Chinese I had spoken as a child this was a trying time because I understood very little of what was going on about me. Of course, my parents spoke English with me but what fourteen-year-old wants to converse with her parents all day! Some of the young people at the church could speak broken English but it was a lonely time for me. Little Gil was my one bright spot.

I had finished my schoolwork and was playing with Little Gil one day. My mother was doing some mending so I asked her to tell me why my parents' engagement had caused problems.

She smilingly continued.

THE STORY

Back in 1928 people's thinking was very different from what it is today. All the Southern Baptist missionaries lived close to each other on the same compound. Their lives were intertwined in many ways and all felt a responsibility to give the best corporate witness to our Chinese friends and fellow Christians. Therefore, they decided that having an engaged couple working closely together as Robert and I were doing at the schools was potentially a bad witness. People might talk! Therefore, it was felt that one of us needed to leave the field until we were ready to get married.

I had been in China for four years at that time and was not due a furlough for another three years. Robert, however, had just returned from furlough beginning a new seven-year term of service. The FMB decided to send me home for a short furlough that would even up our terms of service as well as allow me to purchase my wedding dress in the USA. We would marry upon my return, have our honeymoon, and then come back to Kweilin as a married couple.

I had a lovely six-month furlough seeing my family and friends, sharing about the work in China, and buying new clothes for my life as a married woman. Robert had given me money to buy an engagement ring and I picked out one with three diamonds. I called them "faith, hope, and charity." The women at First Baptist Church in McKinney, Texas, had fun helping me shop, pick out my wedding dress, and pack my trunk. All too soon the time came to leave my family again but none too soon for my return to Robert. I sailed on the Empress of France to Hong Kong where Robert would join me on board as the ship was going on to the Philippines where we planned to honeymoon.

While I was nearing Hong Kong, Robert and some of our missionary friends were already there preparing for the wedding. We were to be married in the Union Church where his Grandfather Lord had preached as a missionary to China in 1847. Because Hong Kong was a British colony and we were American citizens we were required to have both a representative from the American and British consulates present. A British chaplain had to ask a certain question during the service and, of course, we wanted our own Baptist minister and friend, Dr. M. Theron Rankin, to perform the ceremony. So, there were two preachers and two consular representatives officially involved when we made our marriage vows. Robert used to laugh and say how hard it would be to untie that knot!

When we returned to the ship to continue on to the Philippines for our honeymoon we discovered that the captain had transferred us to the Bridal Suite without any extra charge. We spent a pleasant month in Baguio, Philippines at the Pines Hotel and then returned to Hong Kong.

After buying a Model-A Ford we drove back to Kweilin enjoying together the amazing mountain scenery along the way. Chinese custom required Robert to give a big feast in Kweilin inviting all our friends and acquaintances to celebrate his bringing home a bride. Everyone who gave us a gift, no matter how large or small, must be welcome. Some of our students joined in giving one gift but all had to be invited to enjoy the feast! Robert booked the largest restaurant in town for that special occasion. Then we settled down to life in Kweilin as Rev. and Mrs. Robert Bausum.

****

Although life in Keelung had settled down to a routine I was still holding a grudge against God for making me leave America and come to this place where I felt so alone. Little Gil seemed to be my only real joy outside of my piano. After school lessons were done for the day I would play the piano and he would sit near me listening and sleeping. Afterwards we would play together in the way puppies love to play.

Then the unthinkable happened. Little Gil became sick. There was no veterinarian in Keelung so we drove the twenty miles to Taipei to have him treated. We were told that Little Gil was very sick with distemper. The vet told us to leave him there and they would do everything they could to save him but we all knew that distemper was normally fatal. I went back to Keelung with the heaviest heart praying that God would spare my Little Gil.

The next day was Sunday so we could not check on him until after the morning services. As soon as most of the worshippers had left I went back to my dad's office in the church to see if he had any word about Little Gil. Dad's sad face told me the news before he could even speak. Although the vet and his wife sat up all night nursing Little Gil, he had died early that morning.

There are no words to express what I felt that day. My dad and I immediately got in the truck and drove to Taipei to bring home the little body. Dad fixed a nice box and we buried Little Gil on the hill above our rented house. I felt like I was burying my heart with him. For many days, after my schoolwork was done, I would climb the hill, sit by the grave, and ask God why He had not answered my prayer and healed Little Gil. It was a long week of spiritual struggle for me.

The young people at the church understood how broken hearted I was, and about one week later they appeared at our house bringing a little puppy. I immediately told them I did not want any other dog but they suggested I just keep this one until evening. If I still did not want him, I could bring him back to them when we went to the service that night.

That puppy managed to capture and heal my heart during those few short hours. By evening there was no way I was taking him back! He proved to be very strong and adventuresome so I named him Hercules. Very quickly that was shortened to Herky. It was only later that we thought to check things out and discovered that Herky was actually a girl, but the name stuck.

I have already mentioned that the new church in Keelung was holding services every night and people were accepting Jesus each night! It was truly an amazing and moving experience in spite of my own spiritual struggles. I was "required" to be there for every service to help with the music because no one else in that entire congregation could play the piano. Unfortunately, there was no piano so I ended up pumping a tiny little two-and-one-half-octave organ, but at least it helped keep everyone on key. I attended the service each night because of this responsibility, even while I was questioning God. That was a blessing because I continued to hear God's Word preached even as I was involved in a spiritual struggle in my heart. Slowly God brought me back into a right relationship with Him. I realized that I never doubted God's existence or His sovereignty. I was simply mad at Him. In the end I forgave Him, realizing we cannot always understand "why" God allows things to happen, and He forgave me for getting angry at Him! I became more accepting of being in Taiwan and God began to change my heart.

Mom and I were lingering over lunch one day while Dad was away at a meeting. It seemed a good time for her to continue telling me about her life.

THE STORY

Your dad and I were very happy in our ministry and our married life. Of course we wanted a family and were thrilled when we learned that we were going to become parents in March 1931. It was an exciting time. I wrote my family and church back in Texas and everyone sent me the nicest gifts for the coming little one.

The missionary doctor was away on furlough when the time came for our first baby to be born so a British woman doctor came to help me. The baby was large, the birth difficult, and the umbilical cord was wrapped around her neck. Today, if that happens, the doctor will cut the cord before delivering the baby but in 1931 that doctor still believed this was not possible. By the time our little girl made it into the world she had been choked to death. We named her Carolyn Ruth and buried her in a flower garden near our house. March 7 has always been a sad day in our memories.

God is faithful, however, and over the next few years He blessed our home with the birth of your two brothers and yourself. In fact, after George and Howard were born we thought we would have no more children as I was already in my thirties and your dad, as you know, is seven years older than I am. Neither of us could ignore our desire to try to have a little girl - especially after losing our first one. Therefore, in 1936 we decided to try once more for a girl and God blessed us with you - which explains why you are so spoiled!

Perhaps you would like to hear a few more details about your births. We were so afraid that there would be a repeat of what happened with Carolyn that when I became pregnant with George we did not write home to tell anyone I was pregnant. It had been so difficult the first time because everyone was so excited for us. We also decided to go to Hong Kong for this birth as we felt the baby and I would have the best medical care there. Therefore, we went to Hong Kong to await George's birth.

The nurse called my doctor when I went to the hospital but he assumed the wait would be quite a while and delayed his coming. By the time he reached the hospital a nurse had already delivered George.

When it came time for Howard to be born there was a missionary doctor, Mansfield Bailey, living in Kweilin and I gave birth in our house, as I did when you were born, four

years later. God taught me that He is always in control.
Whether things go as planned or not God still works it all
together for our good because we love Him and are trying to
please Him with our lives.

My faith in God's care was tested many times after that,
especially when World War II began. We knew that life in
China would be dangerous and the FMB gave me the option
to take you children and return to the USA. Other missionary
families made that decision but I could not feel that was
God's will for us. Your Dad really wanted us to be in a safer
place, but I told him, "No!" I believed God wanted us to
stay together in China and minister to the Chinese people
as they went through this terrible experience. I told your
Dad that I would stay and take care of him and God would
take care of us all. We did not make such a decision lightly,
though, and promised each other that we would always take
our family and hide in the caves during the air raids. As you
know, that is what we did and God was gracious to bring us
all through it safely.

****

After about a year of renting that house on the hill in
Keelung, Taiwan, my dad was able to build a mission-owned
house near the harbor. We moved in and I thoroughly enjoyed
the view, spending many hours watching the ships come and
go. I knew many by name and found great pleasure in seeing
them leave and then return months later. They came and
went around the world and I would imagine where they had
been and what adventures they might have had.

My beloved Herky had a litter of five puppies some time
after we moved into this house. We were able to find homes
for all of them, but the smallest one I chose to keep. She
was sandy-colored, different from her siblings, and had a
white tip on her tail. I was reading Charles Dickens' <u>The Old</u>

Curiosity Shop at that time so I named my new puppy Little Nell. She and Herky got along fine but, of course, Herky remained the boss.

My bedroom in the new house had Japanese tatatami on the floor. This was a type of matting made from some form of grass woven into about an inch thick 'carpet.' I chose to have this floor instead of a bed and enjoyed sleeping on the floor with my two dogs beside me.

I received my high school education through a correspondence course from the University of Nebraska while in Taiwan. My mom was my teacher. I was still determined to get back to the USA as quickly as possible so my plan was to study the year 'round in order to complete four years of study in only three years' time. We normally spent the mornings studying, the afternoons doing whatever we pleased, and every evening we went to church.

This was at the time when Communism had just taken over the mainland of China and many people had escaped to the island of Taiwan in order to live in freedom. These refugees, for the most part, had left some of their family members back on the mainland. They were lonely, sad and somewhat confused. This made them ready to hear the Gospel about a God who loves them. We had church services every night and two times on Sunday with people accepting Jesus at every service.

I was still the only pianist in the church so, after about one year of pumping that tiny organ, when we moved to our new house I decided to place my beloved upright piano in the church house. It became my habit to spend a lot of time there practicing the piano while my dad worked in his office. Many of the Chinese young people did not have any family in Taiwan so, whenever they were free, they would congregate at the church for fellowship. I gradually became a part of that group. My language skills improved and my friendships grew deeper. Life was not so miserable for me anymore.

It was raining hard one afternoon when my dad was out of town. I had finished school and lunch but had no way to get to the church to see my friends.

"Mom, tell me more about your own missionary experiences before and after you married Dad," I suggested.

THE STORY

When I first arrived in Kweilin, I thought it was the most beautiful scenery I had ever seen. In fact, the Chinese have a proverb that says, "Kweilin scenery is more beautiful than heaven." You probably have some memories of those majestic mountains rising up out of the flat land. However, you saw them mostly as a place to hide from Japanese bombs, I am afraid.

I nodded my head in agreement because what she said was absolutely correct.

I loved the Chinese people from the start. They were very kind and loving even though many of their customs were strange to me. Of course, they had to give me a Chinese name so my teacher picked words that would sound something like my name, Euva Majors. What they came up with was "May Yu Hwa" which means "beautiful jade." It made me feel beautiful!

Three other "old maids" lived in the same lovely little cottage with me. All the Baptist missionaries lived near each other in a walled compound but the rest were families, except for the bachelor Robert Bausum and his mother.

Just a few months after I arrived in Kweilin, armies were marching, conflict was raging, and the beginning of Communism was evident. At the time of my 25th birthday

Kweilin was surrounded by four army generals - warlords all wanting to take our city. We were daily dodging bullets. It was a frightening time but I knew that God had brought me to China and He would keep me safe as long as He wanted me there.

I contracted malaria early in my missionary career and stayed doped up on quinine a good bit of the time. That was not pleasant! However, the joy I found in my ministry outweighed the difficulties. By the time I had been in Kweilin three months, I knew beyond a doubt that I was born to be a missionary.

I quickly discovered that my red hair was a definite asset to sharing the Gospel. Everywhere I went I drew attention because most Chinese had never seen a redheaded person. I loved to play the accordion and I linked these two factors together to help bring people to Jesus even before I could speak much of the Chinese language.

I would stand outside the church house each evening before an evangelistic service playing my accordion and singing. When people stopped to look at my red hair and listen to the music I would say, "Chin jin lai!" (Please come in!) *In this manner I helped fill up the building and many people were able to hear the Gospel for the first time.*

Often in the midst of my daily work I would feel the Holy Spirit nudging me to go and preach. Then I would just walk down the street handing out tracts until someone invited me to sit down and visit. Soon a crowd would gather and I would tell them the story of Jesus. It was so satisfying to see light come into the eyes of people who were living in the darkness of idolatry. You know, Jesus looked on the multitudes and felt great compassion - enough to die for people everywhere. When I saw the life of the Chinese people and how lost they were I wanted to do something for them. That's how I felt when I went to China.

The situation in Kweilin got so bad that your dad took

his mother, who was ill, and returned to the USA in 1926 for an early furlough. The rest of us had to leave Kweilin also, and ended up staying in Canton on the east coast of China for a year and a half. During that time I was able to visit the Philippines and Hong Kong. For a while it seemed as though we could never return to Kweilin, so I began to consider studying Cantonese and staying on the coast to serve the Lord. No matter how bad things were I felt I could never give up China unless there was absolutely no way for me to stay there.

****

I began to want to learn to drive when I turned 15 years old. My dad took me to the capital city of Taipei to get me a learner's permit. To my chagrin, they denied me a permit because I did not weigh enough! The requirement was that one had to weigh at least 50 kilos (110 pounds). I was about 5 kilos underweight. I went home and began to eat everything in sight trying to gain the needed weight to qualify for a permit.

Some months (and pounds) later we went back to Taipei and applied again. All went well and we sat in the office while the man went in the back to issue my permit. When he returned and handed me the little booklet, however, we realized he had actually given me a driver's license, not a learner's permit. I was already 16 years old by Chinese standards because they consider a baby one year old when it is born. Therefore, I qualified for a driver's license. He said nothing about me taking a test or even asked whether I knew anything about driving. My dad knew I could not drive, though, so he began the process of teaching me.

Traffic in Taiwan was a driver's nightmare. There were many vehicles on the roads, people did not seem to know much about rules or regulations, and everyone drove with their hand on the horn, blowing it constantly. It was a challenge for my dad to teach me how to drive and how to drive correctly and safely. To his credit, he was very patient while still being strict.

Although we lived in Keelung, my dad taught several courses at the Baptist Seminary in Taipei that was twenty miles away. I had long since taken up the habit of traveling with him just to have a change of scenery. Therefore, when I began to learn to drive this bi-weekly trip provided some good driving practice time.

The road to Taipei passed through many small villages with people walking all over the road. Dad was afraid for me to be at the wheel when driving through so much pedestrian traffic so we established a driving pattern. On the open road I would drive but at the outskirts of a village I would stop the truck and Dad would take the wheel. He would stop the truck after we passed through the village and I would take the wheel again until we reached the next village. We repeated this pattern over and over, until we reached the capital city of Taipei. Our travel time was longer than normal but I learned to drive!

I never drove anywhere alone the whole time I lived in Taiwan. I did learn the basic skills of driving, however, so when I returned to the USA I was able to get an American driver's license without much problem. This was possible thanks to my brother Howard, who taught me how to parallel park and dared to let me use his car to get some much-needed practice.

While in Taiwan, I had a couple of opportunities to do some teaching. There were a number of businessmen who wanted to improve their conversational English to help them in their work. My dad arranged for a group of them to come to the church and he put me in charge of conversing with them. It was an interesting challenge for a fourteen-year old girl, but a pleasant one.

Another time, a missionary family from a different denomination needed help with their first grade daughter's home schooling. I remember helping her for about six weeks and they paid me for doing it.

When we lived in Baltimore I had already learned that I liked standing before a group telling a story. I clearly remember the first time I had the opportunity to tell a story in Chinese to a Vacation Bible School class. It took a lot of practice and I trust the children understood me but I praise God that He helped me rise to the occasion and give it my best.

Being the only American teenager on the island of Taiwan provided me with many "adult" experiences. When the missionaries gathered for their annual meeting they planned activities for the younger children, but I simply sat in on the adults' business meetings. I remember nothing about what they discussed but I do remember a lot about the way in which they discussed. It amazed me that dedicated Christian missionaries could have such strong verbal disagreements. However, this experience actually prepared me in a unique way for the future God had planned for me.

Every year the Baptist missionaries planned a camp for youth from all over the island of Taiwan. The first year, they talked me into going although I could understand very little Chinese at the time. I was too shy to room with the Chinese girls so I slept in a tent with the women missionaries. I do not have good memories from that camp.

By the second year, however, my language had improved greatly and I wanted to attend the camp. This time I insisted on rooming with the other girls. The one outstanding memory I have from that week took place on the final night. Dr. Y.K. Chang was the preacher for that camp and, on the last night, he gave a strong invitation - not only for salvation, but also for service. The Holy Spirit stirred me to remember the call to foreign missions that I had received at the camp in Maryland when I was ten years old. Now I knew that God was calling again and this time it was specifically to be a missionary to Chinese people.

I went forward recommitting my life. Then Dr. Chang gave opportunity for all who wanted to testify to the reason they had come forward. A long line formed as many youths wanted a turn to share. I suddenly found myself standing in that line. When it finally came to my turn I stood before that large camp gathering and gave my testimony in Chinese. I have no recollection of what I said but only that God enabled me to say it in the Chinese language. It was a strong affirmation of His calling upon my life that remains clear in my memory, even today.

****

I began to prepare for leaving home as I entered my senior year of high school. My choice for a college was to follow my brothers to Carson-Newman College (CNC) located in Jefferson City, Tennessee. George and his wife, Effie, had already graduated and were living in South Carolina at the time. Howard would be graduating in June so neither of them would be there when I went, but I still wanted to follow in my big brothers' footsteps.

When my final exams were completed my dad and I took a trip around some of the island of Taiwan. We visited places I had never seen and I especially remember our stay on the Ah Li Shan (Mountain) in central Taiwan. The mountain was higher than the clouds so when we looked out from our hotel room we saw clouds below us with mountain peaks sticking up through them. It was an awesome view that has remained in my memory. We also saw some tribal people - former headhunters - and I dressed up in some of their costumes to have my picture made. It struck me how much they looked like our Native American tribal people.

All too soon, June 2, 1954 arrived and I was leaving

Taiwan. It amazed me that such a change had come over me in less than three years. I was an angry fourteen-year-old when we arrived with one desire - to leave as quickly as I could. Now, a more mature seventeen-year-old I found myself in tears when leaving. That day at the Taipei airport was indelibly printed in my memory.

I could hardly see to walk up the stairs and find my seat as I boarded the small plane in which I would begin my journey to America. The flight attendant recognized my situation and invited me to come back and stand in the doorway of the plane even though the steps had already been removed. This enabled me to see those who were waving goodbye to me. About thirty feet away on the tarmac stood my parents, many of my Chinese friends and missionary aunts and uncles. They were all singing, "God Be With You 'Til We Meet Again," in Chinese. My tears flowed even faster for I had no idea if I would ever see any of them again until we "meet at Jesus' feet."

The first leg of my journey was from Taipei, Taiwan to Tokyo, Japan. My dad had arranged for an FMB missionary couple to meet and entertain me during my twelve-hour layover in Tokyo. They were very kind and helpful to me. When I was getting ready to board the plane for America I discovered that my bags were overweight. How embarrassed I felt to open my suitcases right there on the floor of the Tokyo airport and do some re-packing! The missionary couple kindly took my extra items and saw that they were mailed to me in the USA. I told them good-bye, boarded the Pan-Am flight, and did something my parents had never done. I flew across the Pacific Ocean.

In those days, the planes flew much slower than today and were much noisier. We had to make one stop on Wake Island to refuel. During that brief stopover, we could walk around the island and I remember how desolate it appeared. That made me wonder why it had been so important during

World War II.

Then we made the long flight on to San Francisco, California. My cousin Mary Catherine and her husband, Joseph Krake, were to meet me there. At first, I did not see them and a most lonely feeling grabbed my heart. However, in a few minutes they came rushing up and it was a joyous reunion. I spent a week in their home and encountered another "first" in my young life.

Joe was pastor of a church and he asked me if I would speak to their Wednesday night Prayer Meeting about the mission work in Taiwan. I had no idea how to go about such a task so I told him I would stand up front and answer questions - and that is what I did. The folks had many questions and I found myself answering with no problem. It was a learning experience which prepared me for other such opportunities which came to me in the future. I have ever been grateful to Joe for daring to ask a seventeen-year-old girl to stand up and share about what God was doing in Taiwan.

When I left California I flew to Dallas, Texas, where my brother Howard met me. We spent some precious time driving around in his car visiting all of our mother's family in Texas. It was good to see Granny Majors and all the aunts, uncles and cousins again. Then we drove on to South Carolina to visit with George, Effie and their seven-month old son, Bobby, whom I had never met.

Finally, our trip ended in Maryland where Dad's family was eagerly awaiting our arrival. My Uncle Ben and Aunt Mildred had agreed to be my guardians while my parents were still in Taiwan so I moved into their house for the remainder of the summer. They helped me get everything ready to go to college and put me on the train for Tennessee at the end of August.

My arrival in Jefferson City, Tennessee, was somewhat traumatic as there was no one to meet me. The only person I saw when I got off the train was a man whom I later learned was a mentally challenged person who just hung around town. Fortunately, he was kind and was able to tell me which direction to walk towards Carson-Newman College. I left my trunk at the station, carried my smaller bag, and trudged up the hill in the hopes that someone would find me and tell me where to go. It was, no doubt, one of the loneliest moments in my young life.

As I neared the college, I saw an older student coming towards me. We exchanged names and it turned out that she had been assigned to be my "older sister" for the first weeks of school. She had actually written me a letter earlier in the summer but we had not made any appointment to meet upon my arrival. Truly, God was looking down on this lonely missionary kid (MK) and caring for my needs. My "sister" helped me find my dormitory and I began to settle in.

The next encounter was with my roommate, Virginia Ann Robertson, from Virginia. She had already taken the upper bunk so I made my bed in the lower one. This worked out well for both of us as Virginia was much taller than I and could climb into the upper bunk much easier. Although we had never met nor corresponded before, we hit it off fine and enjoyed being roommates our freshman year. During our sophomore year we continued to room together with a third roommate, Mary Elizabeth Roane, also from Virginia. The next year Virginia moved to another dorm but we remained friends throughout our college years.

I roomed with Lassie Lou Abner, from Tennessee, my last two years and Mary roomed across the hall. I have lost contact with Virginia and Lassie has gone on to her reward in heaven, but Mary remains my true friend.

****

I decided to major in Bible at college because of my strong sense of calling to be a missionary to the Chinese. My general plan was to finish college, work as long as necessary to earn the airfare, and then return to Taiwan. However, God had other plans that He gradually made known to me over the next four years.

I enjoyed the Bible courses I took and made A's in Greek class but, after some time, I realized that to be an effective missionary I really needed to attend seminary also. There I would study many Bible courses so I began to think of changing my college major. A thoughtful professor counseled me in this decision and suggested that I could be an effective elementary school teacher. I changed my major to Elementary Education as this seemed to be the way God was leading.

Because of all the requirements for a teaching degree I soon learned that I would need to spend one summer in school to make up for the time lost in following a different major. I planned accordingly and, with two semesters of summer school, was still able to complete my degree in the normal four years and graduate with my class. Looking back, I realize what a wise decision this was and how much it was in keeping with the gifts that God had already given for me to develop.

College was an interesting experience for me in many ways. First, I had to learn how to be an American again. In fact, the culture shock of returning to America after three years in Taiwan was greater than I could have imagined. My friends in Taiwan were refugees from Communism and their focus in life was to know God better and serve Him more effectively. I found most of the college students very materialistic in their interests and provincial in their worldview. I am sure God placed friends, especially Mary, in my life to help me make these tremendous adjustments.

I joined the Volunteer Band because I was a "mission volunteer." We were all interested in being missionaries and shared many precious times together learning about opportunities for service as well as reaching out and serving in the community around us. Along with the Baptist Student Union, we helped plan occasional chapel programs about missions and I was one of the speakers when the whole school gathered for chapel.

I had many "extra" opportunities to share about my experiences in Taiwan as an MK. I was often the speaker at women's groups, church services and even the Kiwanis Club once. I enjoyed this kind of sharing more each time. It was not long before I could laugh at the fears I had felt in California about sharing in that small prayer meeting group.

I had opportunities to travel to other cities in Tennessee to share about missions, sometimes even being excused from classes to make extended trips. One time I participated in a School of Missions in north Georgia. This was a week of mission emphasis in an association. A number of missionaries came and each one spoke in a different church each night. It was an honor for me to be one of the "missionaries."

Another memorable speaking engagement was the time I was the featured speaker for an associational Woman's Missionary Union meeting in Knoxville. It was a banquet and there were many women there. One woman who came up to me after I spoke was a missionary from Taiwan whom I knew. She was so kind in her comments about my speaking and later wrote a letter to my parents telling them how well she thought I did. It made me grateful that she would encourage me in such a way.

My parents returned from Taiwan for a furlough at Christmas time 1955. My brothers and I all went to Annapolis, Maryland for a reunion with our parents. I had not seen them in a year and a half, but it had been more than four years since George and Howard had seen them. Although our parents had originally planned to return to Taiwan, various circumstances brought them to the decision that it was time to retire.

They lived in a rented house in Jefferson City for about eight months when they first returned from Taiwan. I lived with them for one semester. Later, they bought a house in Mt. Vernon, Kentucky and officially retired from the Foreign Mission Board in April 1958, when my dad was sixty-five years old.

There were many other experiences and memories from college that I could write about. I made many friends, some of whom I still know today. The most outstanding experience - the one for which I am most grateful - is one of the major reasons God took me to Carson-Newman. It was there that I met my best friend.

****

My life's dream since I was a very young girl had been to marry and have four children. I wanted two girls and two boys like my parents. When I went to college one of my major goals was to find a husband. I soon began dating one young man and we were getting along quite well. However, when we came back from the Thanksgiving holidays we decided to break off our friendship since he did not have a call to foreign missions.

I occasionally dated other guys and was always on the lookout for "the" one but, somehow I never seemed to find him. Couples began pairing off and I was beginning to get discouraged. I knew God had called me to be a missionary but I also had this dream of being married with four children. I began to wonder if God was going to bring those two goals together.

I never seriously questioned God's call upon my life for foreign missions after that experience at the camp in Taiwan, but in early 1957 I wrestled with God over where He was calling me to serve. I had interpreted His will to be a clear call to work with Chinese people. After all, I could now speak

Mandarin and I could relate well to Chinese. It all seemed to "fit" but was this His will or mine?

For some time I prayed about this matter and thought of all the possibilities. Perhaps He was calling me to go to Africa instead. This thought seemed to disturb me. Africa was the last place I would want to go! Also, there was the matter of a husband. Was God calling me to be a single missionary? Heaven forbid! Finally God brought me to my knees in prayer and I made a solemn commitment to Him. "I will go where you want me to go - even Africa. And if you want me to go without a husband then I will be a single missionary." With that settled, my heart knew peace.

The next morning I was studying in the library when Bobby Evans came up and sat down across from me to study. I guessed right away, however, that he had something on his mind other than studying for he had his book upside down! Finally, he got up his nerve and asked me if I was going to the piano concert the next night. I told him I was planning to go with my girlfriends and he asked if I would plan to go with him. I agreed and he took his upside-down book and left.

I had known who Bob Evans was from the time we were freshmen together, but we had no special relationship. He had his group of friends and I had mine. Occasionally our paths crossed at some church meeting but, for the most part, we had had little contact over the two and one-half years we had been at Carson-Newman. I was not aware of him having much interest in foreign missions although he was a ministerial student and active in the Ministerial Conference. As I talked with my roommate, that night, I was rather regretful that I had agreed to go to the concert with him because I had never envisioned Bob Evans as a "possible candidate" for husband!

We did attend the piano concert the next night, however, and I thoroughly enjoyed the music. Later, I learned that Bob did not really like that kind of music but it was a way to have a date without spending any money because it was a lyceum program and already paid for with our tuition. That worked well for two poor college students! He walked me back to my dorm afterwards and, before telling me goodnight, he asked if I would have breakfast with him in the morning. I said, "Yes," and we have been having breakfast together ever since!

We were together constantly from that day. Although we had none of the same classes, we spent all the time outside of class together. As we became better acquainted, I learned that Bob had also been feeling the call to foreign missions. He had attended a conference in 1956, where he heard some tapes concerning the five missionaries who were killed by the Auca Indians in Ecuador. God had touched his heart and prepared him to be just "the one" I had been waiting for.

We began dating in late February 1957 and, by April, Bob had given me his high school ring and we were going steady. Across the whole campus, our friends considered us "an item" and rejoiced because we made a good couple. This was an affirming expression and we were grateful to have such caring friends.

We debated whether to continue going steady or not during the long summer break. However, we decided that we could write letters and that would be a good way to deepen our friendship so I kept wearing his ring. When school was out Bob headed to Manchester, Kentucky to sell Bibles and I headed to Richmond, Virginia to be a summer missionary with the Southern Baptist Home Mission Board.

I had already been a summer missionary for the Maryland Baptist State Convention during the summer of 1955 after my freshman year. Working in Vacation Bible Schools that summer had certainly been an eye-opening experience. I worked mostly in small churches where the pastor was bi-vocational and the members were few. Over the course of those ten weeks, I filled every position that there was in a

Vacation Bible School. At one small church I was actually the principal, pianist, secretary, and teacher – all rolled into one. These experiences stretched my abilities and ingenuity and I learned much about depending on God.

Often, I had the opportunity to share about mission work in Taiwan. I was feeling comfortable in talking about missions by this time but I always gave the same message using the same outline. Each talk pretty much covered all I knew to say about mission work in Taiwan.

However, after I had spoken to one church group the pastor appreciated what I said so much that he asked me to share again on Wednesday night. I agreed but had no idea what I would say. I thought I had said it all on Sunday! The Lord was gracious and taught me how to tell the stories of individuals, and make the message more specific instead of just a general overview of the work. How good God is to set before us a challenge and then gently guide us in the way to accomplish it!

My second experience as a summer missionary, this time with the Home Mission Board, was in 1957. I was sent to Richmond, Virginia where I served at a Rescue Mission. Again I was involved in Vacation Bible Schools, but there were also times of just watching the children play and joining in with their activities. It was more of an inner city ministry so the children came from very different backgrounds than the ones I had worked with in Maryland. At one point, I became very dissatisfied because I had to be on the playground and just play with the children. The woman who was overseeing the work called me into her office and "read me the riot act." She told me I had the wrong attitude. I had felt that teaching was the only important responsibility but she reminded me that everything we do is a witness for the Lord. I asked God to help me change my attitude and added another lesson learned to my maturing process.

While I was in Virginia and Bob was in Kentucky that

summer we wrote each other EVERY day. I was staying with a family in Richmond and I remember sitting in my room writing Bob all about whatever I had done that day. Then I would walk a couple of blocks to the nearest mailbox and send my letter to him. I guess he was doing the same thing because every day when the mailman delivered the mail there was a letter from Kentucky for me. It is significant how much we learned about each other through our letter writing that summer.

At the end of the summer I went to stay with my parents in Mt. Vernon, Kentucky until it was time to return to college. Bob hitchhiked over to Mt. Vernon and stayed a few days after he finished his work in Manchester, Kentucky. It was so good to see him after the ten weeks of separation! All too soon, it was time to return to Tennessee for our senior year at college.

Rev. and Mrs. Robert Lord Bausum – July 23, 1929

English Class Dorothy taught in Keelung, Taiwan – 1952
Dorothy and Robert in front row

Euva, Dorothy and Little Gil
at home in Keelung, Taiwan – 1952

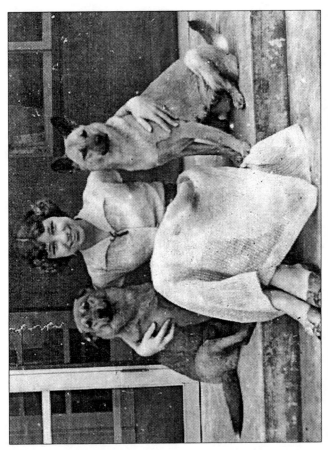

Little Nell, Dorothy, Herky - Keelung, Taiwan
— June 2, 1954

The Fourth Seven Years

1958-1964

*O*ne Saturday, when our college campus was quiet, I asked Bob to share with me about what life was like growing up in his family.

THE STORY

Well, I was born in Rome, Georgia, on October 27, 1935, to Clabe and Rachel Evans. They already had three sons: Gene, Clabe Jr. and Chandler. Four years after my birth they had another son, Lewis, so there are five of us boys in the family. I became quite sick with some kind of digestive problem when I was little. No doctor seemed to be able to find out what was wrong with me and it seemed as though I would die. However, God had other plans and somehow I survived and grew to be a strong healthy boy.

My parents were not practicing Christians so I did not attend church as a young child as you did. However, when I was about nine years old my older brothers began attending the DeSoto Park Baptist Church and I tagged along with them. There I heard the stories of Jesus for the first time. I was immediately interested and continued to attend Sunday School and worship services for God had been preparing my heart.

When I was eleven years old, I answered God's call to salvation and gave my heart to Jesus during a tent revival. There was a lot I did not understand and my parents were not able to encourage me in spiritual things so for the next few years I had many doubts about my salvation. Often I would find myself going back down to the altar to be saved "again." Finally, one of the older Christian men in the church helped me to understand that our salvation is a matter of faith. We simply have to trust that what God says He means. After that, I began to grow in my spiritual life.

*I really praise God for men and women in the church who encouraged and discipled me in my Christian life. By the time I was a teenager I was teaching a Sunday School class and helping with the Royal Ambassadors (*a mission study group for boys*). Although I had worked part time during my school days, when I finished high school I went to work full time with no plans to further my education. At that point, no one in my family had ever gone to college and I certainly had no plans to go either.*

God had other plans, though. It was during that year that He spoke to me about serving Him full time. I could not imagine what I would be able to do but my pastor encouraged me to be a preacher and God confirmed that idea with His calling. Then my pastor began to talk with me about going to college. That also seemed impossible but he spoke with the church leaders and the church agreed to help me financially to further my education. So, I came to Carson-Newman as a "preacher boy."

I made friends with Buddy Crowder and others and we often went out preaching on the streets of Jefferson City as well as in the city jail. These friends were on fire for the Lord and so was I. Although I had once heard a missionary from Japan share about his ministry I never gave any thought to becoming a foreign missionary myself. I have already told you how God spoke to me in 1956 through those tapes from Ecuador and it was then I surrendered my life for foreign missions. That is why I attended that conference at Lake Louise, Georgia this past April, also. My family will probably think I am crazy but I am leaving it to God to help them understand.

I have been a member of the Ministerial Conference since I came to CNC. That is why I never joined the Volunteer Band after I felt God's call to missions. Did I tell you that this semester I have been elected to be the Conference president? It is an honor I never thought would be mine! I really enjoy

*going out on the preaching trips. Sometimes I lead singing
and sometimes I preach. It is such a joy to serve the Lord!*

I was glad he had shared all this with me as it helped me
to know Bob more intimately. It also really confirmed in my
heart that Bob and I would one day be married. He loved
me. I loved him. And God had called us both into foreign
missions. It only remained for Bob to "pop the question."

I went on that School of Missions in north Georgia soon
after this talk. There I met an Associational Missionary
from San Jose, California, by the name of Roy Young. He
was very kind to me and I felt led to share with him about
the budding relationship I had with Bob. I even confided in
him that I believed Bob was going to ask me to marry him.
Before I left Georgia, Roy Young gave me his address and
offered me an open-ended invitation. "If you two get married," he said, "come to California and serve as summer
missionaries in my association. I will request you by name
if you want to come."

****

Bob and I had been at the library studying one evening
in October, and he had walked me back to my dormitory.
It was still early so we found a couch in the parlor and sat
down to talk for a while before having to say good night. It
was then, with couples all around on different couches and
our dorm mother keeping a close watch on all of us, that Bob
asked me if I would marry him. He was dreaming of going to
the Golden Gate Baptist Theological Seminary in California
and wanted to know if I would be willing to teach school
while he attended seminary. I had known that this moment
was coming and I had my answer all ready. The part about
teaching school in California was new to me but I knew that
I wanted to marry Bob Evans wherever he was going. My

answer was a definite "yes," and that settled it.

I have always felt humbled by the unconditional love that Bob has expressed for me. He loves to tell how he "watched" me for many months before getting up the nerve to ask me for a date. Somehow he thought I would turn him down. Perhaps because I was an MK and somewhat different from other Americans he could not really judge how I would react. Anyway, I thank God that Bob finally got up the nerve to ask me for that first date and, in time, to be his wife.

I went to Bob's home in Georgia to meet his family in November 1957. I always remember how his mother gave me a warm welcoming hug when we met. It was a pleasant weekend, but we did not tell them we were talking of marriage.

I do not remember exactly when we told my parents but I do remember their reaction. They were both so very pleased! They had met Bob during the months they lived in Jefferson City and they liked him. In fact, when my mother learned we were in love she said, "I fell in love with him before you did, Dorothy!"

I spent that Christmas with my parents in Kentucky and then rode the train down to Georgia to spend some time with Bob's family. He had bought an engagement ring and it was my Christmas present that year. Our college graduation date was set for May 30, so we planned our wedding for June 1, 1958.

I wanted to make my own wedding dress so I spent my last semester of college in front of a sewing machine. The dress would never have been completed without help from my friend, Mary. Even at that, the night before our wedding my mother-in-law-to-be was sewing the many buttons on the long sleeves for me. I made a chart at school for one hundred days before our wedding and stuck it up over my bed in the dorm. Each night I would color in a square before sleeping, marking another day closer to becoming Mrs. Bobby Dale Evans.

I was given several bridal showers by friends at school, but the shower I remember most vividly was one at which the "givers" were not present to give their gifts. The Woman's Missionary Union (WMU) women across the state of Tennessee had been very kind and thoughtful to me as an MK throughout my college life. Often I would receive a letter with $5.00 in it or a package with something to brighten my day. One women's group decided to give me a shower when they heard about my upcoming wedding.

I had never met these women and they were not in Jefferson City so they came up with a unique idea. When they met for their monthly mission study they each brought a gift for my wedding shower. Then they packed all the beautifully wrapped gifts into a large box and mailed it to me. When I received it at college, I gathered my closest friends around and they watched me open all those wonderful gifts. I wrote a thank you note to the group but I hope one day in heaven to meet those precious ladies and be able to thank each one in person!

Finally, school ended. Graduation was on Friday, May 30. The next day we drove down to Georgia and, on Sunday, we were married in the DeSoto Park Baptist Church. We chose Bob's home church for two main reasons. My parents lived in Mt. Vernon, Kentucky, but I had no strong ties to that church because I had only visited there a few times. My brother George and family were living in New Orleans, Louisiana, and Howard was in New York. Bob's family, however, all lived in Rome, Georgia. It just made sense to be married where all his family and friends were together. My family was going to have to travel wherever we had the wedding.

Our wedding was a small family affair. I wanted my dad to marry us but we also wanted Bob's pastor, Rev. Emmett Smith, to have a part in the ceremony. Since I had no sister I decided to ask my roommate, Lassie, to be my maid of honor.

I asked my brother Howard to walk me down the aisle and give me away since my dad was standing down front as the preacher. George was to be the soloist and Bob's dad was to be his best man. In the end, George had throat problems and could not sing so Bob asked his fellow Bible salesman, Tom McBride, to be the soloist. A girl from the church played the piano for us.

My brother George and Bob's brother Gene served as photographers. Clabe Jr. and Lewis were ushers. Chandler and his wife, Jean, were living in Washington State and could not attend. Gene's wife, Murlyne, and my friend Mary served the refreshments at the reception that was held in Bob's family home.

We had secretly planned to drive my dad's car when we left on our honeymoon so the brothers were not able to decorate it and embarrass us. This also left our car behind for my dad to pack while we were gone. We drove only as far as Cedartown, about thirteen miles from Rome, and spent the night. The next day we returned to the Evans family home for a brief visit. Then we got in our car and left for California.

In keeping with Roy Young's invitation, we had earlier written him of our wedding plans. Then we applied to the Home Mission Board (HMB) to be summer missionaries in San Jose, California. Brother Young wrote the HMB requesting us by name and that is where we were assigned. Our honeymoon was driving across the country from Georgia to California.

My dad had carefully planned the trip for us with the number of miles we needed to drive each day in order to reach California by Friday evening. We were able to make several sightseeing stops at the Grand Canyon and other places of interest along the way. It was a blessing that the HMB paid our travel expenses to get us to our mission field in California since we were very low on cash. Our plans were to stay there for Bob to attend seminary so the HMB did not have to pay our way back home to Georgia. We always figured we saved them about $75.00.

****

Serving as summer missionaries in the San Jose Baptist Association (now The Santa Clara Valley Baptist Association) was both interesting and challenging. Every week or two we moved to a different home where we stayed as guests. During our time in an area we would take a census to discover new prospects for the church, teach in Vacation Bible School, or do anything else that the local pastor needed us to do. For a couple of those weeks we helped in the associational Royal Ambassadors and Girls' Auxiliary camps. We served as teachers and helpers but also dorm counselors. This meant that Bob slept with the boys and I slept with the girls. Some honeymoon! It was great to be sharing about Jesus, though, and we became acquainted with many leaders in the association through that summer's ministry.

Experiences can vary widely when you stay in other people's homes. So many people generously opened their homes for this newlywed "missionary" couple and blessed us with much love and care during that summer. Two examples can show the extremes with most of our experiences falling somewhere in between.

We stayed with a family who ate so scantily that within the two weeks we were there I became very ill and was diagnosed as anemic. Another family was away on vacation and simply left their house keys for us to "make ourselves at home" and "eat anything in the refrigerator or freezer" that we desired. It was the first time we had been alone in a house since our honeymoon drive across the USA.

We looked for a house to rent when our ten weeks with the HMB were completed and I began to look for a job. I had agreed to teach school and help put Bob through seminary but first I had to find a job and that was not as easy as we had hoped. Time was growing short and we began to despair that I would find anything so we started to look around for jobs other than teaching. I did not seem to fit the qualifications at any place where I went for an interview. Our faith in the Lord's guidance was being tested.

Then, just before time for school to start, I went for an interview at a small school in a town called Coyote, south of San Jose. The principal probably took one look at me and thought, "A brand new college graduate with no teaching experience and she certainly doesn't look like she is twenty-one-years old!" But he was a kind man and willing to give me a chance. I think he was also somewhat desperate. I was applying to teach fourth grade but he hired me when he learned I also had some music skills. How we praised God for His provision! Bob began his studies at the seminary and I began teaching school.

Bob commuted back and forth from San Jose to Berkeley that first year of seminary. By the second year, however, Golden Gate Seminary had moved to its new campus located in Mill Valley across the Golden Gate Bridge. For his final two years of seminary studies he rode back and forth across this famous bridge, Tuesday through Friday, every week. He always car-pooled with friends as I drove our car to my job.

The name of the school where I was teaching was Encinal, located in the town of Coyote, a thirty-minute drive from where we lived. It was a small school with one class for each grade - kindergarten through eighth grade. I normally had about twenty-five students in my fourth grade class each year. The teachers were friendly and a good spirit existed between all of us. Because Coyote was a prune growing area our students were either from homes of those who owned the orchards or homes of those who picked the prunes. This meant that in every classroom there was quite a divergence of backgrounds and, often, of abilities. Many of the children spoke Spanish in their homes and, therefore, less-than-perfect English. I loved all the children and truly enjoyed the years I had the privilege to teach in Encinal School.

We had found a tiny one-bedroom house to rent in San Jose and settled down to our busy lives. Bob left home about 6:30 each morning and I left about an hour later. He rode north and I drove south. We returned home between 4:30 - 5:00 in the afternoon and I prepared supper while Bob studied. It was our practice, in those early days, for me to have supper ready by 6:00 p.m. when "Amos and Andy" came on the TV. We would sit in the living room eating and laughing. Other shows we enjoyed from time to time were "Wells Fargo," "The Rifleman" and, of course, the Evening News. There was not much time for TV watching, though, as Bob had his studies and I often brought home papers to grade while there was always the housework to keep up as well.

One of the churches we had served in during that summer of 1958 was the Alum Rock Baptist Church. Since we were living not far from there the Lord led us to join that fellowship when we got settled. The pastor, Rev. Clyde Price, was especially encouraging and helpful to Bob during our early years in California.

Another church where we had helped in Vacation Bible School was the Calvary Baptist Church in Redwood City. About one year after we arrived in California their pastor, Rev. Phil Tilden, asked Bob to come and be his Associate Pastor. This was an outstanding opportunity for Bob to work side-by-side with an experienced pastor. He learned many important lessons that helped him in the years that followed as he pastored churches and then mentored other young pastors.

We lived in San Jose for one year but we decided to try to relocate closer to our place of ministry when we began attending the church in Redwood City. An apartment in Menlo Park became available and we moved there before school started again in the fall of 1959. This made Bob's drive to the seminary somewhat shorter and my drive to school somewhat longer but we were closer to the church and, therefore, more readily available for our responsibilities there.

****

After we had been married about five months I suddenly came to the realization that since I was happily married it was now possible to begin fulfilling the other part of my childhood dream – children. Bob and I talked about it and I suppose I "talked him into it" but we did agree that, God willing, we would go ahead and begin our family. If I could become pregnant by November then our firstborn would arrive during the summer. I could still fulfill my promise to Bob to work so he could concentrate on his seminary studies. We began to pray for a child.

By Christmas, we were confident that God had granted our request and a visit to the doctor in January confirmed it. We could expect our first baby on August 22, 1959. I had to inform my principal soon and see what the school's policy was towards a pregnant teacher.

Interestingly, Encinal School had never had a pregnant teacher before so there *was* no policy! The principal met with the school board and they decided that I could complete the year of teaching as long as my doctor approved. However, this caused them to realize that they did need a policy and, before long, they put something down in writing. In the future, a teacher could teach until she was five months pregnant and then she would need to take a leave of absence.

For my pregnancy, however, I was able to teach until school was out by which time I was already seven months pregnant. My students were all very excited that I was going to have a baby. Bob took me for an evening drive near the end of the school year and we ended up in Coyote. I was completely surprised that my students (with the help of their parents) had planned a baby shower for me. It was in the home of one of my students and was such a happy occasion for all of us.

During those months of waiting for the arrival of our little one, Bob and I discussed what we would name her/ him. Along with my childhood dream of four children was the added detail that they would come in the same order as my parents' children: girl, boy, boy, girl. I had given much thought to what I would name my first child while still in college and I already had a firm choice. Gratefully, Bob agreed, so if our baby were a girl, we would name her Jenny Ruth and call her by the double name. I had chosen Jenny because that was the name of my father's sister, my Aunt Jennie, whom I never had the privilege to meet. We changed the spelling from "ie" to "y." The middle name came from my own sister, Carolyn Ruth, who had died at birth depriving me of the joy of knowing her also.

I was so convinced that my first child would be a girl that I had never given a thought to a boy's name. The 1959 January Bible Study in our church was on the Bible book of Mark, held during the early months of my pregnancy. Bob and I decided we really liked that name and if our baby were a boy, we would name him Mark. It took us several more months to choose a middle name that we thought would go well with Mark. We reached this decision through a strange series of events.

Bob had the opportunity to supply preach in a church located near Salinas and we made the hour-long drive down there for several Sundays in a row. Along the roadside were many large signs advertising things to do and places to stay in the coastal tourist town of Monterey. One sign caught our attention and held it during those Sunday drives - "The Mark Thomas Motel." We had found the name for our baby if it was a boy.

When summer arrived and school was out, I began in earnest to prepare for our baby's arrival. It was exciting to collect the things that would be needed. I even made a lining for the basinet with material that had tiny pink roses on it, bordered with pink ruffled ribbon. As I sewed I thought about the coming fall when I would have to leave my baby and go back to school. She was due August 22 and school was scheduled to begin exactly five weeks after that. So I boldly asked the Lord to allow the baby to arrive one week early. That would give us at least six weeks together before I would have to leave her with a baby sitter.

I was so confident that my prayer was logical and reasonable that, when August 15 arrived, I fully expected to go into labor. However, that day came and went with absolutely no sign of the baby's arrival. I began to panic. Each day I reminded the Lord of my request and my reason for asking but each day passed with no contractions. Then the unthinkable happened. The 22nd came and went with no baby. She was not going to be early - she was going to be late! I could not understand why the Lord could not have given me one extra week.

During the early morning hours of August 23, however, I knew it was time to get to the hospital and our baby girl arrived at 12:59 p.m. on that day. It was a Sunday so Bob had to miss church but I was pleased because I had also been born on a Sunday. Our Jenny Ruth weighed 8 pounds 15½ ounces. She had a head full of hair and the nurses enjoyed playing with it and combing it up into a little curl. We were so happy and could not wait to take her home.

The pediatrician came in one day to tell me that there might be a problem. They wanted to observe her for an extra day to be sure everything was all right so I had to leave her at the hospital and go home empty-handed. We returned to bring our baby home the next day and received the good news that all was well with Jenny Ruth. Something had been wrong with her spinal column but it all checked out fine now. "But," the doctor said, "if she had come a week earlier she might have had back problems for life. It is always better for these things to heal in the womb." We truly went home rejoicing. God had heard my prayer but He knew something about our baby that I did not know so He chose to answer my "logical" request in a more appropriate way.

My parents had come from Kentucky to spend a month with us and help when the baby came. It was good to have them there for encouragement and to have my mom in the kitchen for a while. We settled down to learning how to be parents of an infant and I marked each day as it drew closer to the time for school to begin again. Sometimes I would be overcome with the dread of having to leave our baby. God had provided a woman in the Redwood City church to baby sit and we knew that she would take good care of our baby, but I longed to keep my Jenny Ruth close to me all the time.

The weekend before school was to open we had a teachers' day on Saturday so we could all get our rooms in order. I went down to do my job while Bob watched our baby. My heart was so heavy. Then a miraculous event occurred. Sunday night, before school was to start on Monday, there came a terrific rain storm with thunder and lightening. People told us that this was a truly rare happening in that part of California.

My principal called me early on Monday morning and said, "The storm last night knocked so many prunes off the trees that the children will have to help their parents gather the fruit before it ruins. School will not open for another week." I put the phone down and just sat there in awe. God had kept our baby in the womb until she was strong and healthy so she did not arrive early as I had requested. However, He *had* heard my prayer for the extra week with my baby and sent a rainstorm to grant it! That was a most awesome week in my life. To add "icing to the cake," the night before school finally opened Jenny Ruth slept through the night for the first time.

Our lives settled into a routine. We were up by 5:30 a.m. each school day. I often held Jenny Ruth in one arm while preparing breakfast with the other. By 6:15 we all loaded into the car and drove Bob to a nearby church where he met his ride to the seminary. Then I drove to the babysitter's house to leave Jenny Ruth. From there I journeyed on south of San Jose for another day of teaching. It was a busy, difficult time. Some mornings, if Jenny Ruth was still asleep, we would just pick her up from her bed and not even change her diaper before taking her on to the sitter's house. In retrospect, this was an upsetting time for all three of us.

Bob received a call to be pastor of the Ford City Baptist Church in Milpitas after serving as Associate Pastor at Redwood City for six months. Ford City Baptist Church owned an old house for their worship building and there were two apartments on the back of the property. They rented one out to others but kept one for their pastor's residence. In February 1960, we moved from the apartment in Menlo Park to the apartment on the church property in Milpitas. Now I was closer to my school but Bob was farther from seminary. Our days of travel were not yet over.

A dear friend in the Alum Rock Baptist Church, Ann Adams, became Jenny Ruth's babysitter and was a great help to us in many ways during those years when our money was scarce. Because her husband, Ralph, sold children's clothes they often gave Jenny Ruth pretty little dresses which had been his samples. Although we did pay her for watching our baby, Ann and Ralph gave us much more than we were able to give them.

The Ford City Baptist Church was a small struggling group when they called Bob as pastor. They could only pay him $10.00 a week "gas money." It was essential that I continue teaching until he finished seminary. We owned no furniture since we had lived in furnished rented places thus far. Jenny Ruth was still sleeping in a basinet but the Alum Rock Baptist Church had a crib they did not need and gave it to us. Someone else gave us an old kitchen table and chairs. We also needed living room furniture and a bed but did not have money to buy both so we bought a good sofa couch. That was our only bed for the next few years.

The floor in that church apartment was hard cold tile. Our friend, Ann, was afraid when Jenny Ruth began crawling that she would get sick so she went out and bought a rug for our living room. This was just the beginning of our learning how God uses His people to take very practical care of His servants.

Bob enjoyed his studies and serving in the church. It was a learning experience for both of us. He would visit both church members and new people in the community every opportunity he had. He has a gift to pastor and he used that gift to love the people and build up the church. The little church began to grow with the love and care of a pastor, even a very young, inexperienced one.

I had the privilege of being one of two people in the church who could play the piano. Since those early days in the Junior Church in Baltimore I had always taken every opportunity to use my gift in music for the Lord's work. In time, I became a Sunday School teacher and fulfilled other responsibilities of a pastor's wife. We were still very busy and did not have much money but we were happy in the Lord.

****

We made a trip back East to visit our families in the summer of 1960. Our car was not really up to such a long drive so we rode the train. We stopped in New Orleans to visit George and family as he was attending the Baptist seminary there. Then we rode up to Atlanta where Bob's family met us and we spent some time in Rome with them. Afterwards, we traveled to Kentucky and then rode up to Annapolis, Maryland with my parents. It was our joy that August to attend my brother Howard's wedding to his bride, Gwen Jordan. We were able to see all of our family in that part of the country. Then we returned to California to get back in the routine of school and church work. Jenny Ruth celebrated her first birthday and we bought an 8mm movie camera to record that occasion as well as many others that would follow.

We settled back into our routines and Bob was off to a good start in his final year of seminary work when I discovered that I was pregnant again. According to our plans, we wanted three more children but it would have been better for Bob to finish his studies before another baby came. However, we knew that God's hand was in this and the baby-to-be was surely going to be special. I began calling him "Mark." Jenny Ruth was learning how to talk and so I taught her to say, "Mark" when she felt the baby moving in my womb.

Two events stand out in February 1961. Bob had to have an emergency appendectomy and I had to take a leave of absence from my teaching. I worked with my substitute for a short time before turning the class over to her completely. It was good to be at home full time with Jenny Ruth but receiving only half of my paycheck was not so good. The Ford City Baptist Church made contact with the Southern Baptist Home Mission Board and began to arrange for salary aid so they could pay Bob more. This became a reality, according to their plan, and the aid gradually decreased as the church salary gradually increased until the church was paying Bob a living wage. In the meantime, we became very good at counting pennies!

Our second baby was due on May 20 so I was *very* pregnant when Bob graduated from the seminary in late April 1961. It was a relief for Bob to be out of school although he had enjoyed his studies. No more long-distance driving and more time to put into the church work. I was home with Jenny Ruth and looking forward to the arrival of our first son, Mark Thomas. We were happy.

****

May 20 came and went, with no baby. It was a whole week later before baby number two decided to arrive. While I was in the labor room Bob asked me what we should name this baby if it was a girl. Since I had named Jenny Ruth he wanted to name the next girl. That seemed fair and he chose Cynthia Annette. I was still confident that it would be a boy. However, when the baby finally arrived at 6:05 p.m. on May 27, 1961 she was a girl. We were thrilled to have a healthy baby and I knew that God had His reasons for giving us another girl. The two boys I dreamed of would just have to come later.

We brought Cindy home on Memorial Day, May 30, and placed her in the same basinet that Jenny Ruth had used. When Ann Adams, our babysitter, brought Jenny Ruth home our almost two year old ran to the basinet, stood on tiptoe to peep in and exclaimed, "Mark!" It took awhile to teach her to say, "Cindy." In retrospect, it was good to have the girls close together so they could be friends and have somewhat the same interests at each stage of life. God always knows what He is doing!

A few weeks after Cindy was born, my substitute teacher and the entire fourth grade class came to our home to see the new baby. They had made cards for me and rejoiced in seeing my new little girl. What a nice way to end my teaching experience!

That summer we made our first trip to the Glorieta Baptist Assembly grounds to attend Foreign Missions Week. Glorieta is located near Santa Fe, New Mexico, so it was quite a drive. A family in our church lent us their car and also a navy tent so we could camp out and save money. However, when we arrived at Glorieta it had rained hard the night before. Although our tent had a "floor" of canvas, before the night was over the damp ground was soaking through. The four of us were all sleeping in one double sleeping bag - freezing. The next day we located a cabin to rent so we were warm and dry thereafter, although still "roughing it." The trip was worth it because of our ongoing commitment to foreign missions. We celebrated Jenny Ruth's second birthday on the drive back to California.

When I received my final paycheck from Encinal School I decided to withdraw what money I had paid into the teachers' retirement fund. It amounted to $1,000 which we really needed. The first thing we bought was a washing machine - no more dragging dirty diapers to the Laundromat! The other item that I had really missed was a piano.

While living behind the church I could walk out and practice on the church piano but Bob had to be at home for me to leave Jenny Ruth. Now we were getting ready to move to a house and I *needed* a piano. My dad had built up some credit with a piano company in Tennessee when we rented a piano there during my college days. With the balance from my retirement fund and that credit, we were able to order a piano from that company and have it shipped to California. We still owed money on the piano but it was worth it to have one in my home again.

Moving into our own house that year was another of God's many blessings. A family in our church, the Paul Dukes, had owned several homes in Milpitas as investments. They were moving away and decided to sell their properties. They gave us one house. All we had to do was take over the payments. This was truly a blessing from the Lord since we could never have found the money for a down payment. In September 1961 we moved into this three-bedroom house.

Our plan was for Bob to work full-time at the church and

I would do substitute teaching at Encinal. The principal was very kind and promised to call me first when any teacher was absent. However, when I went to teach it meant Bob had to stay home with the two girls and that did not work out very well for him. After just a few times we decided that I could not continue to be a substitute teacher.

Since the church salary combined with the HMB aid was not enough to live on, the only other alternative was for Bob to look for a secular job and become a bi-vocational pastor. He was fortunate that through the kind help of one of our church members the Milpitas Post Office gave him a job driving a mail truck to pick up and deliver mail. He worked for them several years until the church was able to pay a full salary. We still had to get up early each day to get him off to work but at least he did not have to drive across the Golden Gate Bridge daily as before.

****

Gradually, we settled into life in our new house. Bob worked at the Post Office from early morning until mid-afternoon. The rest of the day was dedicated to church ministries. I was also involved with various church activities as our little church always provided childcare. I could just take the girls and go. It was a good time in our lives. We were in our first house, we had two beautiful girls, the church was growing, and we were learning more each day about serving the Lord. That Christmas my parents came to visit, for they had not yet seen Cindy.

It was a busy December at home and in the church. I was exhausted by January. Then I discovered that I was again pregnant. We both felt this was too soon even though we did want two more children. Cindy was only seven months old! It was a difficult time because I felt guilty about not wanting the baby. However, it seemed that I had no reason to feel guilty as it was not in God's plan for that baby to be born into our family. In March I miscarried, which was a very sad experience. Overall, it was best that we not have another child just yet, but a life that had been a part of me was now gone. I grieved for the baby I would never know this side of heaven.

Our spirits were uplifted in April when Bob's mother got on an airplane for the first time in her life and flew to California to visit us. She was worried that I would be depressed and, of course, she wanted to see her son and two granddaughters. Her visit was "just what the doctor ordered." She was a joy to have in our home and we did many fun things together. She also sewed dresses for our little girls, which was a blessing. All too soon, she returned to Georgia and to Bob's dad, who never got on an airplane in his life.

We planned another trip that summer to Glorieta for Foreign Missions Week. On this trip we did more sightseeing. First we drove down to Glendora, California, and visited with my cousin Mary Catherine, her husband, Joe Krake, and their children, as well as her sister, June Powers, and family. We journeyed on to New Mexico for the conference and it was at this time that we met Charles and Erica Morris, missionaries to Malaysia.

They shared with us how much Malaysia needed pastors and that became a matter of prayer for us. On the return trip to California we drove through Salt Lake City to see the Mormon Temple and other sights. It was a good time for our little family and Bob and I were especially excited because I was experiencing morning sickness throughout the whole trip. It was time to begin planning for the arrival of Mark Thomas.

We were still committed to becoming foreign missionaries, but I could never forget that my missionary parents had lost a baby because of inadequate medical help in China. We did not yet know where God wanted us to serve overseas but I had grown up with the firm conviction that I wanted to have all four of my children BEFORE leaving the USA. Each time we went to Glorieta our pull towards foreign missions became greater but our plan was to have two more children before going overseas. Spacing them about two years apart meant that we could not apply for appointment for at least another four years.

It was at this point in my life that an idea took root and gradually became a prayer. In a way I could say that I bargained with God. In retrospect, however, perhaps He was bargaining with me! Anyway, I suggested to the Lord that if He would give us twin boys then we could go on to the mission field much sooner. That seemed logical to me and I was quite sure that God could do it if it was His will.

When we returned from our trip I went for a check up and learned my baby's due date would be March 10. By December, however, I looked like the baby should come any day yet we still had three months to wait! Each month when I went to see the doctor I would ask him, "Could it be twins?" He would listen and then shake his head. "I can only hear one heartbeat. It's just going to be a big boy." It made sense that my third baby would be bigger than the first two who had both been good-sized babies. I kept on praying and reminding God of my bargain.

March 10 came and went with no baby. Jenny Ruth had been one day late and Cindy had been one week late, so it came as no surprise that Mark wanted to be late too. However, I was very heavy and uncomfortable. My doctor sent me straight to the hospital and induced labor when he saw me on the 12th. All indications were that the baby was in position and ready to be born. Bob got me checked into the hospital and then returned to complete his postal deliveries for that day. Judging by the girls' births we both calculated he had plenty of time to finish his mail route and get back before Mark arrived.

As we discovered, however, an induced labor goes more quickly than otherwise and Mark Thomas came into the world screaming at the top of his little voice long before his dad returned from his postal duties. When the nurse told me I had a boy I thought my heart would burst with joy, but she had a further surprise for me. "You are going to have another baby," she said. God had truly given me twins but the doctor's face told me there was trouble. He explained that the second baby was breech and the first choice would be to wait until it turned itself around. Then I would go into labor again to deliver number two.

Unfortunately, this baby's heartbeat began to slow down indicating that it was in distress so the doctor decided to put me to sleep and give the baby some extra help. Two things I remember clearly from those moments before the gas took effect and "put me under." The doctor spoke gently saying, "We'll do the best we can to save the baby." My own thoughts were a prayer to God that He would intervene and protect this little one.

Bob must have returned to the hospital about this time and asked the nurse, "Has the Evans baby been born yet?" She smiled and said, "The first one has," and Bob almost fainted. Then he had to sit and wait for news about the second child.

When I woke up, someone was pushing me down the hall on a gurney and the nurse was saying, "You have another little boy and he is just fine." Bob remembers seeing the babies and realizing that the youngest one had had quite a struggle to make it safely into this world. My doctor, a fine Christian man, told me later, "It was God who saved your baby's life."

When Bob visited me later that evening, we recognized that the first baby had had a name since before Jenny Ruth was born. Mark Thomas had finally arrived. But we did not have a second name picked out. Therefore, just as we talked over Cindy's name in the hospital, once again we were in the hospital choosing a name - this time for "Twin B." Since the boys were twins, and we had already named "Twin A" Mark, we searched for a name that would match. We decided on Michael for a first name and, without too much more discussion, we agreed that David would make a good middle name. It was no time before they became "Mark and Mike" or "M&M" as we loved to call them.

As I lay in my hospital bed for the next four days, it was as though I was floating on "cloud nine." I had brought a book to read but never opened it. My heart was so full of rejoicing over God's blessings that I needed nothing else to help pass the time. I was just full of amazement. God had given us two precious girls and now He had answered my prayer and completed our family with twin boys. Truly, He is a great and loving God!

****

Jenny Ruth and Cindy were so excited when we brought the twins home. It was their understanding that we had brought them each a baby! Although Cindy was only twenty-two months old and Jenny Ruth was three years and seven months, they both became great helpers with their new little brothers. They enjoyed going to get things for me and were good to sit beside the boys and pat them while I prepared bottles, etc. Repeatedly, I was grateful that the girls came first and the twins last!

Life certainly was a lot busier with four children all under four years of age. Bob was still a bi-vocational pastor and there arose some problems within the church fellowship. It was a most discouraging time and we began to question whether the Lord wanted us to stay in California.

That summer, with Mark and Mike not yet six months old, we drove our own station wagon back east to visit our families - my parents in Kentucky and Bob's family in Georgia. There was an ulterior motive for this trip, also. We were looking for another church that Bob could pastor! He preached in view of a call at a church in Georgia and although the folks were very nice and seemed to like us, the call never came. It was time to return to California, so back we went.

Soon after we returned, on top of our personal confusion, the city of Milpitas condemned the old house that the Ford City Baptist Church had bought before we came. The church had to move out. The Lord led us to purchase a piece of land in a new housing district but before we could build there was a period when we had no church building. We met in a high school for a few weeks and then rented a Union hall on Sunday mornings. Evening services were in a church member's home with the nursery across the street in our home. Meanwhile building plans were drawn and finances arranged for the new church building.

Mark and Mike turned one year old during this time and, according to society, it was time for their first haircut. However, I loved their light brown curly hair and was reluctant to have it cut so I kept putting off that "fateful day."

One Sunday evening while the nursery was in another church member's home, the women caring for the children decided to give our twins their first haircut. It is to their credit that they saved those precious curls in carefully marked envelopes so I would know which curls belonged to which boy. The ladies explained to me later that they thought we could not afford the haircuts so what they did was done in love, but it took a great deal of help from the Lord for me not to be angry over that incident.

Looking back over this unsettled time in the church's life, we can see how the Lord used these difficult circumstances to accomplish great things for His glory. We broke ground for the first building on a windy March Sunday when

Mark and Mike were about one year old. A Christian builder, Allen Barnes, oversaw the construction of the building but the church members joined in and did much of the work under his direction.

It was a time of excitement as well as forging deep relationships among the members. The church changed its name to Park Victoria Baptist Church because the property is located on South Park Victoria Drive. When the building was completed there was a special dedication service. By this time, the church membership had grown to where they were fully supporting Bob as their pastor and he no longer worked at the Post Office.

We made our third trip to Glorieta in August 1964, just before the church building was completed. Our family was complete, the church was growing, and we had helped them get into their first building. It was time for us to pursue our call to foreign missions.

We did not take Mark and Mike with us on this trip. They were seventeen months old, just learning to walk, and it would have been difficult for us to attend the conferences and take care of them. Jenny Ruth and Cindy were old enough to be in their own classes at Glorieta so we left the boys with a church family who loved them dearly and drove once more from California to New Mexico.

It was on this visit that the Lord spoke to us again, this time through Harold and Ann Clark, missionaries to Malaysia, about the needs in that country. We knew very little about Malaysia but we knew God wanted us to go where we were needed.

****

Bobby Dale Evans – 1949

Rev. and Mrs. Bobby Dale Evans – June 1, 1958

Rachel and Clabe Evans Sr., Bob's parents - 1967

Bob and his brothers: Back row – Clabe Jr., Chandler, Bob (1987)
Front row – Lewis, Gene

FIVE TIMES SEVEN YEARS

1965-2000

When we returned home from Glorieta, we began the process of applying for appointment under the Southern Baptist Foreign Mission Board. This required us to each write a lengthy autobiography, one page for each year of our life, as well as locate quite a few people who were willing to be references for us. As the process moved along, in early 1965, we had to have thorough physical, as well as psychological, examinations before we could receive final approval.

The doctor discovered a polyp in my colon during our physicals and the FMB required the removal of this before I could have medical clearance for appointment. However, the doctor's report was so encouraging that they agreed to fly us to Richmond, Virginia for ten days of orientation <u>before</u> our appointment as missionaries. It was a great privilege to stay in the famous Jefferson Hotel for that occasion. We met missionaries who were already serving in various countries as well as new appointees, like ourselves, whose careers we have followed over the years.

The FMB's faith in my medical situation was justified. The polyp proved benign, we received medical clearance and, on March 11, 1965, in Richmond, Virginia, we were officially appointed missionaries to Malaysia. That was a most meaningful service that my parents were able to attend. Dr. Baker James Cauthen, Executive Director of the FMB, and our friend from Kweilin days, observed that I was the fourth generation of missionaries in the Bausum family.

Everything moved very quickly after that. Bob resigned from the church effective May 1, 1965. They gave us a warm and loving farewell that will always live in our memories. The theme for that day was "For Evans' Sake" and they showered us with love, prayers, and gifts as we moved forward to obey God's call upon our lives. It was very hard to leave those dear people who had been so much a part of our lives for the past five years!

We packed our belongings for shipping and then headed back east to tell our families good-bye. That was an adventuresome trip, to say the least. We had car trouble before we ever got out of California and again just outside of Rome, Georgia. We had to leave that old station wagon by the roadside for one of Bob's brothers to later rescue and dispose of for us.

We borrowed a vehicle from another brother and traveled to Texas for a reunion with my mother's side of the family. Then we gathered with all the Evans clan in Rome for our final days before leaving. My parents were with us throughout these farewells.

In early June we flew out of Atlanta, returning to California where we spent a few days with old friends before boarding the S.S. President Roosevelt bound for Asia. We had so many friends from Park Victoria Baptist Church come to the dock in San Francisco to see us off that other passengers on the ship thought we were some kind of VIPs. We were so excited to be going but it was so hard to say good-bye knowing there were some of these friends whom we might not see again on this earth.

****

Our ship sailed under the Golden Gate Bridge and headed out to the open ocean. We stood at the railing transfixed, watching America fade into the distance. As we turned around to head for our cabin Bob, Jenny Ruth, and I began to feel queasy. We battled seasickness for the next three days until our stomachs got used to the constant rolling motion of the ocean. Interestingly, the three younger children did not seem affected at all!

Life on that big ship was actually a lot of fun. They had childcare during the morning hours when all four of our children could be in classes where they had various activities for their age level. This gave Bob and me some free time each day to do other things. Bob tried taking Japanese language lessons and I enjoyed reading from the library. The children all napped in the afternoon but later we would play shuffle board on the deck with them or just walk around gazing at the great expanse of the Pacific Ocean.

Our family ate dinner at the first seating because we had small children. The meal was served about six o'clock followed by a second seating at 8 o'clock. There was plenty of nightlife on the ship even for a family with young children.

After dinner there was usually a Walt Disney or other movie suitable for the children to watch. There were other planned activities. I especially remember the costume party. I dressed Mark and Mike in their sisters' dresses, scotch-taped ribbons on their heads and took them as twin girls. Jenny Ruth and Cindy dressed up as cartoon characters. None of our children won prizes but it was great fun.

The ship docked in Yokohama, Japan seventeen days after we left San Francisco. It stayed in port a couple of days which meant we could leave the ship. We had contacted a young Baptist couple stationed with the U.S. Army there. They took us sight-seeing on Saturday and we spent the night at their house. After attending Sunday worship services with them they took us back to the ship and we sailed out later that evening.

A few more days and we reached Hong Kong. That was where we left the ship. Before leaving America we had written some of our Baptist missionaries in Hong Kong that we were coming. Somehow, they got the date mixed up and no one met us.

Getting off that ship with all of our baggage and four children was quite an experience. Everyone was carrying all we could and, as we stumbled along, we kept looking for a familiar face. Mark fell over backwards as he was getting on an escalator. A stranger walking behind caught him and helped him regain his balance. Gratefully, that did not make Mark afraid of escalators but he still remembers the incident!

After we made a phone call, a most apologetic missionary met us and took us to a hotel. It was Friday and we were scheduled to leave on Sunday evening. Although we had planned to worship in one of our Baptist churches in Hong Kong, once again there was a mix-up and no one came to take us. Finally, we settled down and had our own family worship in the hotel room. We were glad to get on the plane headed for Singapore that night.

I will always remember our arrival in the Singapore airport at 8:30 p.m. on Sunday, July 4, 1965. As we were getting our baggage and going through customs we could see all the Baptist missionaries who lived in Singapore gathered outside the window waving at us. Although we were grateful to have arrived safely, all four of our children were crying and we were exhausted.

The missionaries quickly took us to our new home and it turned out to be the nicest house we had ever lived in. They had furnished it with borrowed furniture for us to use until we were able to get our own things. We quickly got the children in their beds and settled down to read the mail that had been collecting for us over the past three weeks.

We remember most clearly one particular item in that collection of mail. It was the printed minutes from a Mission Committee meeting in which "it was decided that Bob and Dorothy Evans will study the Mandarin Chinese language." We stayed up quite awhile that evening discussing this decision because it came as a complete surprise to us. Before leaving the USA we had understood that we were going to learn the Tamil language and work with Indian people. We committed the matter to the Lord because all we really wanted to do was His will.

****

When we awoke that first morning in Singapore, Malaysia, it was to a sound we did not recognize. As we looked out on that beautiful tropical morning I remember saying to Bob, "I want to learn the name of that bird." Later we learned that it was not a bird, but a cheechuk, or gecko. There were many new sounds and experiences awaiting us.

The missionaries had stocked our refrigerator with enough food to get us through the next few days. We received a rude awakening as our family sat down to a cereal breakfast. There was no fresh milk available in Malaysia at that time so someone had thoughtfully mixed up a container of powdered milk and placed it in the refrigerator. Our children took one taste of it - and stopped drinking milk! From that day forward, we had to find ways to make the milk taste better or simply demand that they drink a glassful before they could leave the table. It was the first of many adjustments we would make in our eating habits.

Ernest and Marjorie Glass came about mid-morning to give us some orientation to life in Singapore. They brought a young Chinese girl named Ah Hong to watch our children for a few hours. It seemed that Ah Hong was a friend of another missionary's amah (maid) and was looking for a job - hopefully with us. It was with some trepidation that we left our four children with a total stranger and began our missionary career.

Ah Hong turned out to be a "jewel" and we were happy to employ her during the two years we lived in Singapore. She loved our children and they loved her. She kept our house and clothes clean and would do anything else around the house that we asked. It was a great blessing to have her during our language study and early adjustments to life in a different culture.

She spoke simple English but, since we were going to study Mandarin, it was a great help to have her in our home to give us daily conversational practice. She would gently correct us when we used a wrong word or tone. I remember telling her one day that I was going out to get my "head" permed. She reminded me that I was really going to get my "hair" permed. It was a small mistake, perhaps, but an important correction. We needed many other such corrections as our language skills progressed.

Our first weeks in Singapore were spent becoming acquainted with life there and ordering furniture to be made. We had not really owned much furniture in California as most of what we had there had been given or lent to us. So we had a dining room table and chairs, beds, desk, etc. all made to order. It turned out to be cheaper than shipping furniture from the USA. This furniture was so well made that we used it for our entire missionary career, moving it around from place to place as the Lord led us.

Three weeks after we arrived in Singapore we made our first trip to Golden Sands for the annual mission meeting. Golden Sands is the Baptist Assembly grounds located near Port Dickson, Malaysia. We could not imagine, on this first visit, how special this place would become in all of our lives.

The roads were not very good in those days and it took us seven hours to make the drive from Singapore to Port Dickson. (Today it takes between two and three hours.) Our cars back then had no air conditioning, so it was a long hot drive with four children sitting side-by-side in the back seat! As we followed the winding road, Mike became restless and I decided to hold him in my lap thinking his stomach might be feeling a bit queasy. I was right! In just a few minutes he threw up all over the front of the car and me. When we reached the Baptist Assembly Grounds and all the "old" missionaries came out to meet the "new" ones, I emitted an odor that was anything but pleasant - definitely a memorable experience.

The two weeks we spent at the beachside made the

difficult trip worthwhile. Here we became acquainted with Baptist missionaries from all over Malaysia. The meeting included times of worship and inspiration as well as business and planning ministries for the next year. Everything was new to us so we sat and listened and learned. Our children had Vacation Bible School while we adults were in meetings. Afternoons were spent on the beach that truly does have "golden" sand. We took Ah Hong with us and she put the children to bed at night while we had our evening meetings followed by times of playing games and sharing.

One historic event occurred while we were staying at Golden Sands. On August 9, 1965, Singapore withdrew from Malaysia and became an independent nation. How well we remember reading the news in the paper the next morning and wondering what it meant for us. We had visas for Malaysia. Would we be able to get back into Singapore? How would relationships be between the two countries? Our mission work had always been in both areas as though they were one. What would the future hold? Only time would tell. When we returned to Singapore, however, we had no problem getting back in and we settled down to life in our new country.

The first order of business was to begin language study. Other missionaries, Bill Clark and Ruth Thomas, were also studying Mandarin and we employed the same teacher to work with us. Mrs. Wu was a fine Christian lady who spoke very good Mandarin. She worked with us, using books from the Yale University method of learning Chinese. Although she was a good teacher and we enjoyed talking with her, she probably was not strict enough in requiring us to speak "perfectly." We never really had examinations such as would be done in a school situation.

On top of that, when we would go out on the street and try to talk Mandarin with the local shopkeepers, they would want to speak English with us! We did join a Chinese-speaking church and they were a great help to us as we struggled to learn. However, Singapore was definitely not the ideal place to learn Mandarin and, eventually, the FMB started sending new missionaries to Taiwan for language school before they came to serve in Malaysia and Singapore.

Language study was especially difficult for Bob as he was starting from scratch. It is very difficult for an adult English-speaker to learn Chinese because it is a tonal language and has no alphabet. Bob worked very hard, at least eight hours a day, throughout the two-year course. He preached his first sermon in Chinese after one year of study and that was quite an accomplishment.

I had spoken Chinese as a child growing up in China and had re-learned it while living in Taiwan as a teenager. When we arrived in Singapore I could understand a lot of Mandarin but my tones were not very accurate and my vocabulary needed to increase. This background in the language turned out to be a real blessing for me because it soon became evident that I could not spend eight hours a day studying as recommended.

Jenny Ruth began first grade at the Singapore American School in August and we enrolled Cindy in the Baptist kindergarten connected to Calvary Baptist Church. That left Mark and Mike to spend each day with Ah Hong while Bob and I walked up the hill to the study house where we studied with Mrs. Wu.

This all seemed to be working out well until one day when I had to scold Mark for something he had done that was not allowed. Our almost-three year old son looked up at me and declared, "When you go to the study house I can do it!" Being the strict disciplinarian that I am, I could not allow that kind of attitude to continue. It was obvious that Ah Hong would let the children do anything they wanted as long as it did not hurt them physically. Her "discipline" was simply to follow them around and keep them out of harm's way.

Bob and I talked it over and decided things must change. From then on, I only went to the study house for a few hours each morning to study with Mrs. Wu and did the rest of my studying at home. When I was at the study house, Bob stayed at home and studied the best he could while watching the boys. After I returned, he would have the rest of the day to be at the study house. This worked out well and got our boys' discipline back on track. Whenever we had somewhere to go in the evening, we knew the children would be safe with Ah Hong but we did not leave their daily discipline to her anymore.

After we had been in Singapore for about a year, we decided to get a dog for the children to enjoy. We found an adorable Japanese Chin puppy and bought him for 50 Singapore dollars. He was black and white full of energy and very smart. The children named him Tuffy. We allowed him to be both an indoor and outdoor dog as he learned his manners very quickly. He brought a great deal of joy to our home until we left Singapore and could not take him with us. At that time, we found a buyer who loved dogs and Tuffy went to live in Johor Bahru, Malaysia, which is just across the causeway that connects Singapore and Peninsular Malaysia.

****

We joined the Singapore Baptist Church initially to help improve our Mandarin but it truly became our home church while we were in Singapore. In the years that followed, whenever we returned to Singapore we naturally went back home to this group. When we joined them in 1965, it was a small struggling group which met in a rented terrace house - part of a row of houses which are all attached forming a long row. It was a two-storied house so Sunday School classes were upstairs and the worship service was downstairs.

We hoped that by taking our children to a Mandarin-speaking church at such a young age they would learn to speak Mandarin as I did as a child. However, when they were in their Sunday School class the teacher would teach the lesson in Chinese and then, while the other children did written work, she would re-teach the lesson in English to our children! On top of that, they were not hearing Mandarin at any other time in their daily lives as Ah Hong also spoke English to them. Our hope for them to become fluent in the language never became a reality.

The members of Singapore Baptist Church were very kind and loving to our whole family. We had the joy of helping them move towards having a building of their own. While we were members there, they bought a piece of property nearby and began to collect money to build a "proper" church building. Bob had the privilege of helping the men clear the property of bushes and vines and, to this day, those men remember the young American missionary who worked alongside them cutting bushes and sweating to make way for the building that was coming.

It was in this church that Bob preached his first sermon in Chinese and they all listened patiently and congratulated him profusely. I had the privilege of giving a talk for their Woman's Missionary group which helped me with my language skills as well. We formed a close friendship with the new pastor, Chiang Wei Sin, and attended his wedding. He and his new wife then moved into a small room in the back of the rented terrace house where the church met.

On Sunday evenings, we took our family to the Calvary Baptist Church for Training Union and evening worship services so our children would hear English. During those two years in Singapore, Bob also had many opportunities to preach in other churches in English. The missionary men often led the Lord's Supper in different churches, as there were very few ordained Chinese pastors in Singapore at that time. Therefore, although language students were supposed to focus on learning the language we managed to become involved in various opportunities of service besides.

The two years of language study and living in Singapore flew by quickly and the Lord moved us on to another location where we would be "on the job" full time.

****

We had been in Singapore about three months when we received a telegram from my dad. In brief telegraphic language it informed us that my mother had inoperable cancer and ended with the Scripture reference from Philippians 1:21. Looking it up, we were reminded of the Apostle Paul's words as he faced death, "For to me, to live is Christ and to die is gain." Thus began a most difficult year in our lives.

My dad wrote weekly with updates on the various treatments the doctors tried to help my mother. There were "up" days and "down" days as her body battled this dreaded illness. My brothers and their families were able to visit her from time to time. Two of her sisters, a brother and a niece came from Texas to spend some time with her also, but Bob and I decided it would not be possible for me to go.

We had the small children to think of. Also, we did not really have money for the airfare. Then we thought, since all four of our parents were still living we could not go back for each one in a similar circumstance. Therefore, we made the decision for me not to go. Because of that, I wrote my mother a letter every day from the time we received the news of her illness until the Lord took her Home.

There were times when I felt really helpless and sad but our missionary friends and Chinese Christians upheld me in prayer. We never tried to call and chat with her because my mother was hard of hearing and overseas telephone calls were expensive.

Just days before her passing, my brothers and my dad called to talk with me but by then my mother could not talk. She knew I was on the phone, though, and sent her love. After that phone call, I wired some flowers to her and my dad later told me she hugged those flowers, briefly, just before she died. It was her good-bye to me.

Fighting this cancer was a battle that my mother lost on September 3, 1966. There was a meaningful service held in Kentucky at my parents' home church, First Baptist Church of Mt. Vernon. I sent a telegram that was read at this service.

Heavenly music, today is more fair
Since our dear mother is singing there.

Then her body was taken to Annapolis, Maryland for another service in my dad's home church, College Avenue Baptist Church. She was laid to rest in the Hillcrest Cemetery that had formerly been my Uncle Fred's farmland. Many Bausums are buried there.

I think only Jenny Ruth had much of a memory of her Grandmom and we spent some time explaining to her where Grandmom was now. The other children listened but Jenny Ruth grieved some in the way a seven-year old can grieve. This was the first of our parents to pass away and was a reminder to us of some of the cost of being on the foreign mission field.

Life went on, as did the grieving process. I took great comfort in remembering two important facts. My mother understood why I could not be at her side because she had been a missionary in China when her father died. Among her last spoken words to us when we were leaving the USA was that we were her "favorite missionaries." Her life, love, and faith would continue to be an inspiration to me throughout my missionary career.

My dad returned to Mt. Vernon, Kentucky and lived alone

there for another year. Then he sold that house and moved to Annapolis, Maryland, where he stayed with his brother, Fred, and his wife, Ivy Belle. They were very gracious to provide him a home for the rest of his life.

His brother Ben's wife, Mildred, allowed my dad to use an old garage on their property as his office. There he set up his files of books, magazines, stamps, etc. and there he typed letters and worked on various projects. It gave him his own space and gave Uncle Fred and Aunt Ivy Belle plenty of time alone in their own home.

****

When we attended that first Mission Meeting at Golden Sands in July 1965, we once again met up with Charles and Erica Morris. They had returned to Malaysia after we saw them at Glorieta in 1962 and felt God's leading to move to Sabah, East Malaysia to help begin Baptist work in that state. All during that meeting, they talked excitedly about how the work was growing and about the need for more workers. Most of the missionaries were not very interested in moving to East Malaysia as people considered it a "backwoods" sort of place. However, as we listened to the Morrises God laid East Malaysia on our hearts.

By the time we were beginning our second year of language study, the Morrises suggested that we pray about moving to East Malaysia to take their place when they went on furlough in 1967. They asked the Mission for money so that our family could make a trip over there to see if that was God's place of service for us. When our whole family made the visit to Sandakan, Sabah, in East Malaysia, on the island of Borneo, we knew immediately that we could call this place home. We returned to Singapore to complete our language study and prepare to move. This was why we had come. This was why we had spent these two years studying

Mandarin. It was exciting!

Jenny Ruth entered the second grade in 1967 and Cindy left the Baptist kindergarten to begin kindergarten at the American School where Jenny Ruth attended. In March, when the boys turned four, they were allowed to enter the Baptist kindergarten. We took them all out of school in August of that year, however, when we made the move to Sabah. Movers came and packed all of our furniture and belongings to be shipped to the island of Borneo. We had tickets to travel on the same ship with our freight.

The day we left Singapore was both happy and sad. It was hard to say good-bye to our friends, especially Ah Hong, but we were happy to be out of language school and going to our first assignment. We had to ride a small boat out to the big ship anchored in the harbor - the SS Kunak. That experience was quite harrowing as we had to climb down and climb up rope ladders that were swaying as the waves rocked the boat. Each child was handed from us to deckhands who then carried them to a place of safety.

Once on board, the trip was relaxing as there were few passengers aboard the freighter. It took four days to sail from Singapore to Jesselton (now Kota Kinabalu), the capital city of Sabah. We were there a few days and then traveled on the same ship around the island to Sandakan, stopping in Kudat on the way. It was an interesting trip where we experienced many new sights and sounds.

On September 4, 1967 we arrived in the Sandakan harbor where Mr. and Mrs. Tsui See Chung met us. They were a strong Baptist couple helping with the new work. The Morrises had already left for the USA so we moved into the house where they had stayed. It was a wooden house built up on stilts, as are many Malaysian houses, because of the heavy monsoon rains and possible flash flooding. Our three-bedroom living quarters were upstairs and the downstairs had been turned into a worship area with two small Sunday

School rooms. There was also a small lending library in one of these rooms. Our eight-year-old Jenny Ruth devoured almost all the books in that library and grew spiritually because of her love for reading.

Soon after we settled into our Sandakan house, we entered the girls in a local school called Sung Siew Primary School. Classes were from about 7:30 a.m. until 1:00 p.m. It was an Anglican Church school and most of the teachers were local. In fact, at that time primary school teachers were not required to do any teacher training. They simply completed high school and then became teachers in the primary school. The teachers taught in the English language but most of them had very poor English. Along with the language inadequacy, there was also a difference in philosophy of discipline. The first year was very difficult for our girls but things improved some by the second year.

We found a private play school, conducted by an English woman in her home, and enrolled Mark and Mike. They would attend for about four hours each morning. The school was small and they made friends easily with the other children but they would come home exhausted from each day's activities.

After lunch, we required all four children to rest and then I would give them some school lessons from the Calvert School in Baltimore, Maryland. We knew that without these extra lessons they were not getting the quality of education they needed to be "up to speed" with American schools. It made a full day for the children but we kept time for them to play also.

We did not try to get another dog but ended up inheriting two kittens so we still had pets. One year Bob bought two little bunny rabbits at the market and we kept them for a while before they met with misfortune. Our children's love of pets, however, ended up being a bad thing. Mike had often been sick in Singapore but he grew worse after we moved to

Sandakan. He had various respiratory problems and was on medication most of the time. It was some years later before we finally learned that he was allergic to many things - especially cats, and possibly longhaired dogs!

****

Although the Sandakan Baptist Gospel Centre consisted of a small group of believers, the work was growing and new believers were added to the fellowship from time to time. A significant addition occurred in April 1968.

I mentioned earlier how our Jenny Ruth loved to read the library books that belonged to the church. Through that process, she learned a great deal about how people found the Lord and dedicated their lives to living for and serving Him. We did not realize how much she was learning until one particular evening.

I was preparing supper and the girls were getting their showers after a hot afternoon of playing. Suddenly, Jenny Ruth came running out of the bathroom exclaiming,

"Mommy, I just asked Jesus into my heart!"

I was thrilled and a little taken aback. We had no idea that she was thinking so deeply about spiritual matters. We talked a moment and I told her how happy I was for the decision she had made. Then she ran back into the bathroom to complete her shower and I heard her say to Cindy,

"I am a Christian now and you should become one too!"

Gratefully, Cindy did not try to "just make a decision" because her sister did but waited until later when she, too, came under conviction of the Holy Spirit. But I was thrilled to hear Jenny Ruth sharing her faith so quickly after accepting Jesus. Later, before bedtime we talked some more about her decision and what it would mean to her long-term.

We helped Jenny Ruth prepare for following the Lord in baptism and, in April, we had a baptism service for Jenny

Ruth and Elizabeth Ho, a girl who had been attending the Gospel Centre for some time. Since there was no baptismal pool under our house, we used the swimming pool at some friends' house and that is where our eldest daughter gave public testimony to her faith in Jesus Christ. She was almost nine years old.

From the beginning, it had been the plan to establish a Baptist Church, buy property and build a church building in Sandakan. While the Morrises were still there, a piece of property had been located just a few blocks from the missionary house. Amazingly, in this Muslim country the government had given the land for a Baptist church. When we arrived, the property was little more than a mud hole for water buffalo to soak in to escape the tropical heat. However, while we were there we were able to get the land filled so that when there was money for a building the land would be ready.

The Gospel Centre had established a building fund from its beginning. In addition, money was requested from Southern Baptists in the USA through the Lottie Moon Christmas Offering. Every year in Southern Baptist Churches across America money is given for foreign mission work around the world. Sandakan was granted 25,000 US dollars from this fund and, added to the money the local Christians gave, was enough for an initial church building in God's timing.

Bob spent a great deal of time while we lived in Sandakan dealing with an architect and with government officials. Plans had to be drawn and application made for government approval. Things do not move fast in Asia and there were many delays before everything was in order and building could begin. By that time, we had already left Sandakan and another missionary couple, Herbert and Frances Holley, was there to oversee that part of the church planting and development.

****

While we were living in Sandakan, my dad made a trip to Israel and then came on to Malaysia to spend some time with us. We turned Bob's office into a bedroom for him and enjoyed having him as part of our family for the last eight months we were in Sandakan.

My dad could still speak Chinese fluently and he jumped right into the ministry with us. He took a turn preaching and was good in relating to the folks and helping to build relationships. His "brand" of Chinese language was a bit different from what is spoken in Malaysia but it did not take the Malaysians long to tune their ear to his accent and understand him well.

We made a trip to West Malaysia in August 1968. There we had the joy of taking my dad to Penang so that he could see John George Bausum's grave and walk the streets his father, William Henry Bausum, would have known as a child. That was an awesome experience for my dad and one that he treasured the rest of his life.

Then we traveled to Golden Sands, near Port Dickson, for our annual Mission Meeting. My dad went with us and helped teach the children in Vacation Bible School while the missionaries conducted business. Children and missionaries all loved him. Many still remember his visit and talk about him to this day.

My dad was always the type of person who could find a way to solve a problem. If this method did not work he would try that method - until he was successful. I remember two interesting examples of this while he was with us in Sandakan.

One day, a string broke in our piano causing a certain note to no longer function. There were no piano tuners in the whole state of Sabah at that time. A man would come from Singapore once a year to tune all the pianos in East Malaysia. I was bemoaning the fact that we would have a broken piano key for many months to come so my dad put his ingenuities to work and came up with a solution.

Using some pink raffia string made from palm fiber, he managed to re-connect the string to the hammer so that the note would play again. It did not look very attractive, and we laughed a lot over his "invention," but it worked until the piano tuner came again and made more proper repairs.

For Christmas 1968, we were working on a play that the children would present for the church. We needed a star to move across the stage so the wise men could actually follow it as it moved. My dad fixed up a pulley and two wires, attaching a large sparkling golden cardboard star to it.

On the night of the performance, he stood behind the curtain and worked the pulley at the proper moment to make the star move while the brave little wise men, gazing upward, followed it. Unfortunately, the star caught a bit and did not move smoothly with the result that the star was actually following the wise men! It was, however, another of my dad's unique and memorable inventions.

In early 1969, he went by himself to Tawau, Sabah, to spend a week becoming acquainted with the tribal work in that area. Charles and Erica Morris had gone there when they returned from furlough in 1968 and they welcomed my dad's visit. He joined in ministry with them traveling to some of the areas where Karen Burmese Baptists held church services. In later years, he loved to talk about that experience and the wonderful people he had met in that most eastern part of East Malaysia.

While my dad was in Tawau, Bob and I decided that I should take the children and fly on to the USA to have Mike seen by an American doctor. Therefore, when my dad returned from Tawau we were already gone. I had done the sorting and packing of our things but left it for Bob and my dad to handle the crating and storing of everything. That was a big job and I was glad that Bob had his father-in-law to help.

When everything was in order, they left Sandakan and flew to Hong Kong for a few days. From there they traveled to Taiwan where they visited for more than a week seeing most of the country as well as many of my dad's old friends. Brief stopovers in Japan and Hawaii completed their two weeks of sight-seeing and they parted company.

Dad flew to Los Angeles to visit three of his nieces who were living in the area. Bob, meanwhile, flew on to Milpitas where the children and I were reunited with him after almost a month of separation. Thus ended our first term on the mission field and we began our first furlough in the USA.

****

Dorothy and Mike, Bob and Mark, Cindy and Jenny Ruth
Sailing from San Francisco- June 15, 1965

Tuffy – Japanese Chin

Mark, Jenny Ruth, Cindy, Mike – Singapore, 1966

Sandakan Baptist Gospel Centre – Sandakan, Sabah

While we were still new missionaries, the Mission had voted to pay Bob's way to take an orientation trip around the country of Malaysia. His visit to East Malaysia laid the foundation for our future ministry. On that trip he stopped in Kuching, Sarawak, the little country of Brunei Darussalam, and Jesselton, Sabah. He kept a diary so he could share with me his impressions of the places he visited.

The strongest impression he received was towards the city of Kuching. Baptists had no work in the whole state of Sarawak at that time but Bob wrote in his diary that he believed God would have us to plant a Baptist church in Kuching one day. Later, we answered the call to follow the Morrises in planting the Sandakan Baptist Church so this "call" to Kuching was "put on hold" but not forgotten.

After moving to Sandakan, however, Bob encouraged our Mission to investigate the possibility of Baptist missionaries entering Sarawak. Along with a Chinese Baptist layman, C.B. Tsien from Sabah, Bob and Harold Clark visited Kuching to talk with a local man who was willing to help Baptists pursue this idea. The result was that our Mission submitted an application to the Sarawak Government for Baptists to place two missionary couples in that state. Then we waited.

Everyone was surprised when the approval was received from Sarawak in early 1969. Somehow we all thought it would take a long time. Then, the question was who should go? When permission is given to grant a visa there is usually a time limit within which someone must be prepared to enter the country.

It became evident that Bob and I were the only ones interested in moving to Kuching but we were due to take our first furlough in June 1969. We were willing to make the move immediately but the Mission decided it was not wise to begin a new work just before returning to the USA. Therefore, they communicated with the Sarawak government that we would be coming after our furlough and we trusted that they would still allow us to enter.

That was when the idea came up for us to take our furlough a few months early. If we left Sabah immediately, we could return in one year as opposed to waiting another six months before leaving, thus making our entrance into Sarawak delayed by one and a half years. This idea was approved and we made plans to leave. Since Mike continued to be so sick, we decided that I would take the children on to the USA as quickly as possible while Bob and my dad made a more leisurely return trip.

It was hard leaving our friends in Sandakan but we knew we were making the right decision. The Holley family would be moving to Sandakan soon so the church would not suffer because of our leaving. We had spent two years in language study and nineteen months in church planting and developing. It was time for our first furlough and we left Malaysia excited about returning to Kuching and starting a brand new work there.

Because the children and I had gone ahead of Bob, we stopped in California and visited with our friends in Milpitas until Bob joined us. Some of our church friends, Bill and Pat Patterson, were on vacation and allowed us to stay in their house while they were away. It was a real blessing for the children and me to have a "home" during those few weeks while we waited for Bob.

The Park Victoria Baptist Church members were all so kind to us. It was a great homecoming. I took Mike to see our former pediatrician but he was not very helpful so we looked forward to our complete furlough physicals for a more comprehensive diagnosis. Fortunately, his problems cleared up to some extent after arriving in the USA and we were able to have a good visit with our friends in California.

****

Our first item of business in the USA was to purchase a car. After a pleasant visit in Milpitas, we headed south to Los Angeles, taking our children to Disneyland. As school was still in session, the crowds were smaller and we had a memorable experience there. At the same time we visited with my cousins who lived in the area. Then we headed east visiting friends and family along the way. We had booked a missionary house in Anniston, Alabama, for our furlough year. It was not far from Rome, Georgia, where Bob's family lives so we were able to see them often throughout our year in the USA.

The idea of "missionary houses" was just becoming popular at this time. Churches would either buy or be given a house for this purpose. Usually a group of ladies would then outfit it with everything a family would need such as furniture, linens, etc. All the missionary family had to do when they arrived was unpack their suitcases and they were "home." Because a local church provided the house, the missionaries also had the privilege of becoming members of that group for the time they were stateside. This gave them a "home church" to attend, serve in some ways, and where their children could enjoy the benefits of USA church life for one year.

We always found these houses to be beautifully decorated and comfortable, providing all we needed and more. It was a great blessing to be the recipients of this type of ministry each furlough throughout our career.

The Parker Memorial Baptist Church provided the house where we stayed in Anniston. We had many precious experiences being members in that fellowship and continued a relationship with that church through most of our career. The house was conveniently located within walking distance of the elementary school. How well I remember that first morning when we watched the children walk down the street to school - two first graders, a third grader, and a fifth grader.

After their less-than-ideal school situations in Sandakan, it was an exciting day for all of us.

I was a bit upset that the school insisted our boys be in different first grade classes. I had assumed they would be together. It turned out, however, that the school's policy was for the best. Each of them excelled in his own class and they were not competing with each other. It also enhanced their already individualistic traits and helped them establish their unique personalities apart from each other.

My dad came to stay with us most of that furlough year. The missionary house had a full basement and he set up his own space down there. It was a good arrangement and gave him many opportunities to share with his missionary grand-children. He made some trips away from Alabama but we were always glad to see him return to our home.

At Thanksgiving, my brother Howard and family rode the train from Maryland to Alabama and spent two days with us. George and his family drove over from Kentucky and we had a glorious family reunion with only our mother missing. Several of Bob's family members were also able to visit us during this furlough as we stayed so close to Rome, Georgia, where they all lived.

Furlough was a time for sharing about missions - what was happening in the country where we had been for the past four years. Bob took advantage of many invitations to travel to various parts of the country speaking in World Missions Conferences. I did not take any out-of-state assignments during this furlough because the children were in school and I needed to be at home with them. However, I had many invitations to speak nearby and we both thoroughly enjoyed sharing about what God was doing in Malaysia.

One of our great concerns during this furlough was to discover why Mike had been sick so often and to get some treatment for him so that we could return to Malaysia and begin the Baptist work in Kuching, Sarawak. We saw a number of doctors, ran various tests, and prayed a lot. In the end, it was determined that he was allergic to many things both in food and in the air. He began taking regular desensitization shots. For a time they seemed to be helping, although he continued to have some problems.

Because we had left Malaysia in March, we were due to return exactly 12 months later. That would put us leaving before school was out and we did not want to deprive our children of one full year in the USA school. Therefore, we contacted the FMB to request an extension to our furlough until June. They denied our request.

Shortly after this, we were talking with Mike's doctor about our return and he became very upset. He said if he had his way we would NEVER take Mike back to Malaysia! This was quite disturbing to us and we told him we would be going back anyway. Then he replied, "Well, let's give him a few more months on the shots to see if he improves." At our request, he put that in writing and the FMB granted us an extension on our furlough - for medical reasons. Truly, God works in mysterious ways!

This further delay, however, raised another problem. It had already been a year since the Sarawak government had granted visas for Baptist missionaries to enter that state. We had requested a delay while we took our furlough and that had been granted. Now, this situation with Mike raised the question again. Would they be open to a further delay? Once again, Mike's doctor wrote an official statement that we could not yet return to Malaysia for health reasons. This was forwarded to our missionaries on the field who informed the Sarawak government. The Lord went ahead of those contacts and they granted us permission to delay until June to pick up the visa.

As the time drew near for leaving the USA, we began to realize it would be more difficult this time than the first time we left. Everything was new then and we were excited.

Furthermore, the children were younger and really did not understand what it meant to leave their friends. Now they did understand and it was not easy for them. Missionary Kids (MKs) have to learn the unpleasant lesson of always being torn away from friends and the familiar and heading into the unknown. This is not necessarily a bad lesson to learn, but it is a painful one.

Finally, everything was packed, the good-byes all said, and we boarded the plane for Malaysia. It was no longer feasible for the FMB to send missionaries by ship because of expenses. No more could we enjoy leisurely weeks on the ocean creating a break between the sad good-byes and the new experiences awaiting us on the other side. Now we flew from one country to the other in a matter of hours. Before we could stop crying from the good-byes the plane was setting down in Singapore and we were being greeted by old friends. It was an emotional roller coaster.

****

From Singapore, we once again took a smaller steamship over to East Malaysia. First, we landed in Jesselton (now Kota Kinabalu) and spent a few days with fellow missionaries serving there. When the SS Kimanis arrived from Sandakan carrying our household goods, we boarded that ship and sailed down the west coast of Borneo to Kuching. In this manner, we arrived in Kuching together with all our household goods. This made going through customs easier.

Our ship actually anchored in the open waters outside the Kuching River very early on the morning of June 23, 1970. I remember clearly that my heart was full of doubts as we waited for the customs officials to clear us and for a smaller boat to come and take us up the river to Kuching town. We had never started a church in a city where there was no other Baptist church. What should we do? Would we know how to go about it? As I read in my Bible that morning, the Lord spoke to me from Acts 9:6 –"Go into the city and it will be told you what you should do." That verse was a great comfort and encouragement to me in the weeks that followed.

When our small boat pulled up to the jetty in Kuching town, seven people met us - the Robert Buntain family of five, and Mr. and Mrs. Teo Whye Tze. These were the only Baptists we knew of in the whole state! There was an immediate bond among us although we were meeting all of them for the first time. We were so grateful to have a few co-workers to join in this adventure with us.

Some of our missionary coworkers had already been to Kuching a few weeks earlier and rented a house for us to use, both as a residence and a church meeting place. After a few days in a hotel, we were able to get our freight unpacked and somewhat arranged and move into our new home. The house was a two-story duplex with a small front and back fenced-in yard. All of our bedrooms were upstairs while the living room dining room and kitchen were downstairs. This was very convenient because for the year we lived there we used the downstairs for church activities. However, we still had some privacy upstairs.

Since we already had seven people whom we knew would come to worship, we planned to have a worship service on our first Sunday in Kuching. June 28, 1970 there were thirteen of us in attendance - six Evanses, five Buntains, and two Teos. We were all excited about the possibilities for a Baptist work in Kuching. Actually, Mr. Teo was not a professing Christian but he was supportive of the work from the beginning.

Our living room furniture could accommodate this first group but the next day Bob went out to buy chairs for the increased attendance we knew the Lord was going to send. He also went to a printer to have some invitations printed. These gave the location and time of meeting for the Kuching

Baptist Gospel Centre. Each place he went in town he also invited people to come and worship with us.

From a furniture shop and a printing shop, two young women began to attend - Eva Goh and Carol Sim. After attending one service, Eva came by our house one afternoon asking questions about the Gospel. Before she left, Eva prayed and asked Jesus to come into her heart. Carol also made a commitment not too long after that.

In August, we went to our Annual Mission Meeting at Golden Sands. It was exciting to share with our fellow missionaries how God was already at work in Kuching. Seeing all the aunts, uncles and cousins again helped us all to re-connect with our mission family. It had been sad to leave the USA but now we truly felt we had come home.

When we returned to Kuching, we enrolled our children in school. Lodge Preparatory School, run on the British school system, was our first choice for the best education available. Unfortunately, this school only accepted children up to nine years of age. Traditionally, British parents would then send their children back to England to boarding schools for their remaining education. Cindy was nine and Mark and Mike were seven, so we enrolled them immediately in the appropriate classes.

Lodge School proved to be a very positive experience for them. It was a small school, meeting in an old house, and had an adjoining empty piece of property. This served as an ample playground for recess and after school activities. Classes were small, with two grades together in most cases, but the teaching ratio of teacher to student was excellent! Although British, the teachers were very kind in recognizing that our children were American. Some teachers made allowances for the differences in spelling and handwriting styles, but Mark remembers failing more than one spelling test because he did not have enough "fervour" in Anglicizing his spelling.

Mark and Mike were just learning to write cursive at this stage and, even today, the influence of that school is evident in the way they form their letters. Mike writes completely like an American with a flowing cursive style while Mark uses a combination of printing and cursive that follows the British form. Cindy had already mastered cursive before entering Lodge School and the teachers did not try to make her change her handwriting. Because of the age limit, Cindy was only able to attend Lodge School for one year while Mark and Mike had two good years there before we had to make other arrangements.

Jenny Ruth, on the other hand, was already eleven years old and could not attend Lodge School. They kindly allowed her to attend for a few weeks but by January 1971 we had to enroll her in a local Anglican girls' school, St. Mary's. This was far from an ideal situation but she gamely went to school and excelled in her lessons. For the most part, I believe the girls were friendly with her and, many years later, I would sometimes meet up with a young woman who would tell me she had been Jenny Ruth's classmate in St. Mary's.

There were two real drawbacks to this school. Although the lessons were taught in English (albeit Malaysian English!) the teaching methods were archaic. Mostly, she sat in classes of 40-45 students and copied information from the blackboard. They had frequent exams in which the students wrote down what they had memorized, with or without understanding. Jenny Ruth always made good grades except in the language class.

Teachers taught in English at this time in Malaysia because Malaya had been a British colony for so many years. However, the Malaysian government was in the process of changing the medium of teaching to the national language, Bahasa Malaysia. Therefore, those who still studied in English had to also study the Malay language and pass an exam in it. By entering the Malaysian school system in

Primary Six (sixth grade) Jenny Ruth was five years behind her classmates in this area. That was very frustrating to her personally and put a great deal of stress on our eleven-year-old daughter.

To make matters worse, according to the Malaysian/British school system, as students finished their primary school education they had to take an extensive exam over everything they had learned throughout their primary school years. Jenny Ruth arrived for that final year of primary school but would have to take the exam over all six years' lessons like everyone else if she wanted to go on and attend secondary school.

Jenny Ruth had no problem facing that exam in the other subjects. She was an outstanding student with a good mind and studied hard to prepare herself and make good grades. In the Malay language, however, there was no way she could catch up on her own because it was a foreign language to her. It became necessary for us to engage a tutor to give her lessons, starting from the beginning, and trying to bring her up to the primary six standard before the exam time in November. To her credit, she studied hard and passed that exam but it was a difficult and daunting experience for her.

Because we knew that Cindy would face the same problem the following year, we sent both girls together to the tutor's house. She lived across the Kuching River so we would take the girls down to the dock, put them in a small boat, and watch them ride across the river. The teacher would meet them on the other side and take them to her house. This was a unique experience that, no doubt, the girls have never forgotten.

****

We continued giving Mike the allergy shots prescribed by the Alabama doctor, but with each shot he seemed to get worse. Finally our Kuching doctor recommended that we stop the shots altogether and Mike improved, immediately. Although he still had allergy flare-ups from time to time, his health was greatly improved and our hearts were comforted that we had made the right decision in returning to the mission field.

We had the habit of reading with our children at bedtime each night. We were reading the children's version of Pilgrim's Progress, by John Bunyan, during those early months in Kuching. One night after our reading, I had tucked the girls in and gone to get the boys settled. As I was going downstairs Jenny Ruth called me to return to their room. "Cindy wants to talk to you," she said.

The story of Pilgrim, as he journeyed through his Christian life, had touched Cindy's heart and she wanted to put her trust in Jesus. I was thrilled to pray with her that evening. The next day she shared with her brothers about her decision and Mike wanted to accept Jesus, too. I put him off because I was afraid he just wanted to follow Cindy. I suggested he think about it and promised we would talk the next day.

In the morning, he brought up the subject again but there was no time before they left for school so once again we postponed the discussion until after our afternoon rest time. While the children were still resting that day we had a visitor. She stayed and talked until well after rest time was over. Mike kept poking his head in trying to get my attention. "I want to trust Jesus," he whispered.

When our visitor left, I could put him off no longer. We sat down together and Mike asked Jesus into his heart. Then, of course, Mark said he wanted to do the same thing. I suggested we wait awhile to be sure it was really his personal decision. However, before we went to bed that night Mark insisted that he wanted to ask Jesus into his heart and so the family circle was completed on August 31, 1970. In

December, we had our first baptism service with Eva, Carol, Cindy, Mark, and Mike giving public testimony to their faith in Jesus Christ.

That first year in Kuching, we did many different things to get the Baptist work started and to let people in Kuching know that there was a Baptist Gospel Centre at 131 Green Road. The Kuching Baptist Gospel Centre was growing in other ways also. Several mature Christians found us and joined the fellowship. They were a great encouragement during those infant stages of the church.

Dr. and Mrs. Theodore Ling, an older Chinese couple, became some of the most faithful. He had been a Baptist on the mainland of China and she came from a devout Presbyterian background. Before long, the K.E. Kuruvilla family began attending our services. They were Indians from an evangelistic background and fit in well with our Baptist beliefs. These two couples swelled our base of long-time Christians while we continued to reach out, winning new people into the Kingdom of God.

The Kuruvillas had three children who became fast friends with our own children. Leela was slightly older than Jenny Ruth, and Raju was about Mark's and Mike's age. There was no one Cindy's exact age but the Kuruvillas also had Liju who was much younger than our children. Along with the Buntain children, teenagers Hamish and Ian, and two-year old Marianna, we had a good group of children in the beginning of the work. They all related well to each other and when new children came to the Centre the circle of friendship was simply enlarged.

With these children coming regularly, we soon began holding Sunday School classes prior to the Sunday morning worship service. There was a class for the younger ones, a class for the teenagers, and an adult Bible Study class. To accommodate this expansion in our activities we had to begin using more of our house for the church. Children's classes met upstairs in some of the bedrooms, and that meant our family had to get up in plenty of time on Sunday morning to make up the beds and be sure the bedrooms were clean and neat.

The next gathering we started was a Thursday night prayer meeting and Bible study. From the beginning, we moved around from house to house rather than always meeting at the same location. Sometimes this made transportation a bit of a challenge but we developed sweet fellowship through these times. It also became a time of witnessing and sharing the Gospel as we met in homes where there were unbelievers.

We soon began a youth meeting on Friday nights as young people were the most open to the Gospel at that time in Malaysia. We used Christian films to help attract the youth and it certainly worked. Often, on Friday nights so many kids gathered that they could not fit inside our living room. Many would stand around outside the windows, leaning forward to watch the movie.

During that first year, we had to replace the screens on the windows twice because the kids unintentionally tore them as they strained to see and hear the stories. We followed these films with recreation times and refreshments. It was a busy, full evening, but many of the future church members came from those Friday night get-togethers.

Besides Sunday School, worship service, Thursday evening prayer meeting and Friday night youth gatherings we sometimes organized special events to extend our outreach. One stands out in memory as being especially large and exciting.

We obtained a copy of the Billy Graham film "Two a Penny" starring pop singer Cliff Richard. Because he was well known, even in Malaysia, it was easy to advertise and get a crowd using his name. Our small group worked together to present it in a public venue as such a magnetic film could not adequately be shown in our living room.

We rented a hall that would seat 300-500 people and printed advertisements to hand out as well as putting one in the newspapers. Two nights were scheduled for the showing and all of us had responsibilities to try to make this an evangelistic outreach. It was a huge success in terms of attendance.

The hall overflowed both nights with large crowds standing outside disappointed they could not get inside. Some of our members were helping seat the crowd while others stood outside in the parking lot and gave Christian tracts to those who could not find a seat.

Only eternity can measure all the impact of such an event for the Lord's glory, but we shared the Gospel with over a thousand people and Kuching residents became aware that there was a Baptist Gospel Centre in town. Some people did accept the Lord that night and some new folks began attending our meetings.

Several months later, a teenaged girl named Doreen showed up at our house wanting to learn more about the Gospel. She had been unable to get in and see the movie that night but had received a tract. Tucking it away in a book, she forgot about it until she discovered it months later. That was when she came to see us and, eventually, she and her sister accepted the Lord.

****

My birthday fell on Easter Sunday in 1971, and it was a great day. We had our second baptismal service baptizing some of the youth who came to know the Lord through the various activities of the Gospel Centre. The Lord was definitely planting a church in Kuching and we were fast outgrowing the rented house on Green Road.

The Mission had allocated funds to buy a mission residence in Kuching using Lottie Moon Christmas Offering money given by Southern Baptists across the USA. We began house hunting. In time we found just what we wanted. It was a new house in a quiet neighborhood built on a cul-de-sac.

There was a spacious living/dining area where we could easily have church groups meet, a kitchen, bathroom, and small bedroom on the first floor. We turned that bedroom into a study for Bob. On the second floor, there were three bedrooms, a bathroom, and a "sitting" room with a small balcony. The yard was fenced in and provided ample space for the children to play.

The Mission agreed to buy the house. We praised the Lord for His provision and moved in during the summer of 1971. This meant that the entire rented house on Green Road was now available for church use and the group began paying the rent for that building. We now had more space for our family and the Baptist Gospel Centre had more space in which to grow.

As we moved into our second year, we began to teach and train the members, looking towards an official organizing of a Baptist church. However, within the fellowship there arose a problem. This greatly threatened any further growth. It began as a disagreement over certain technical interpretations about the Lord's Supper but grew until some members were holding meetings in their own house, detracting from the ministry that was growing at the Gospel Centre.

For quite a few months, the work stagnated and barely continued to exist. It was a disheartening time for us made especially difficult because a good relationship had gone sour. Every day we prayed for God's wisdom to know how to relate in a loving Christian manner. We prayed for the church we were convinced that God was planting in Kuching. There was never an open confrontation between any members and us but, there was an underlying conflict that definitely stifled the work for a while.

In God's timing, He moved some people out of Kuching and the work again began to grow and prosper. By April 1972, the small group was ready to organize into a Baptist church. There was some discussion over what name the new group would carry. Some favored "First Baptist Church" because it was not only the first Baptist church in Kuching but in the whole state of Sarawak. However, the majority voted for "Kuching Baptist Church" (KBC) and that was the name chosen. April 2, 1972, was a great day as 22 charter members signed the constitution establishing a Baptist Church. All six Evanses were proud to be among that historic group.

Our number continued to grow as friends brought friends to the regular activities of the church. We held our first Vacation Bible School and it was a great success. The youth meetings began having other programs than just recreation and film showing. We planned special Christmas programs, presented a musical cantata, and held a church camp.

Some of our young people traveled to Jesselton (now Kota Kinabalu), Sabah, to participate in their statewide Baptist Youth Camp. When the Baptist work in Miri, another town in Sarawak, was beginning the KBC sent a group of young people to help in the initial outreach activities. It was an exciting time - one that God was blessing in countless ways.

From the time we arrived in Kuching Bob had been searching for land on which to build a permanent church building. He found many pieces of property but each was inadequate for one reason or another. Finally, the ideal piece was located on Ong Kee Hwei Road (now Jalan Tun Ahmad Zaidi Adruce) and we bought it with Lottie Moon Christmas Offering funds as well as money our small group had been putting aside each week from the beginning.

The Kuching Baptist Church moved in 1973 from the Green Road house to a terrace house located across the street from the new property. We began to establish our presence in that neighborhood where the church building would eventually be built. There were various complications and delays so in the end, as in Sandakan, we were not the ones to oversee the construction of the building but our joy was in establishing the church that would eventually use the future building.

****

It was necessary for us to place Cindy in St. Mary's Primary School for the fifth grade after her one year at Lodge School. This was a difficult time for her. The method of study, large classes, study of the Malay language, and their less-than-standard English all worked together to make school an unpleasant experience. Every morning she had a stomach-ache before leaving home.

Jenny Ruth had passed the Primary Six final exam and moved on to Form One, which is equivalent to the American seventh grade. She had adjusted to the "ways" of the local school but there was little challenge to her abilities and mind.

Mark and Mike enjoyed one more year at Lodge School but we were deeply concerned about their future education. Logically we should enter them in St. Thomas' School - the boys' equivalent to St. Mary's, but we were aware of the unusual disciplinary tactics sometimes used in local schools. This had not concerned us too much for our well-behaved girls but our boys had a mischievous way about them. We were sure this would get them into trouble with local teachers resulting in a type of discipline that we could not condone. Therefore, we made the decision to home school all four of our children, beginning in 1973. It was a decision we never regretted, although the children may have often wished for different circumstances.

To set up school in our house required some rear-ranging. We moved Mark's and Mike's bedroom into the upstairs sitting room and moved our bedroom into what had formerly been their room. This left the larger master bedroom for a schoolroom. In there we placed a ping-pong table, hung a blackboard and an American flag. All four children sat around the table with plenty of room to spread out their books and papers.

Every morning we began class at exactly 8:00 a.m. with the pledge of allegiance to the American flag, some Scripture reading and prayer. The children all had their assignments and I took turns working with them individually throughout the morning. About 10:30 a.m. we would break for a Physical Education class which Bob led and I would begin lunch. Then we returned to our classroom for the remainder of the morning. Lunch was about 12:30 or 1:00 p.m. and then the children had their afternoons free. This was my time to be involved in church-related ministries as well as do things around the house.

We had a woman who came each morning to help with the housework, washing clothes, etc. Mrs. Foo had been helping us since soon after we arrived in Kuching. She had a sweet personality, a willing spirit, and was a hard worker. Each day she would dust the furniture, sweep and mop the floors, and wash and iron our clothes. She would usually stay until after we had eaten lunch and clean up the kitchen for me although I continued to do the cooking. It was a true blessing to have her help especially after I began home schooling the children.

In 1973, we began planning a trip to Europe. We would be returning to the USA for a furlough in June 1974 and it would not cost us much more airfare to travel to Europe and across the Atlantic than it would to travel the usual route across the Pacific Ocean. Our plan was to spend three weeks traveling to various countries in Europe.

With a family of six, we knew we had to plan carefully in order to finance such an adventure. We purchased a book on how to see Europe using only $5 - $10 a day and began planning our trip. This book contained information about places of interest as well as reasonable hotels/pensions and restaurants. We decided we could save up money for this trip by letting Mrs. Foo go.

Although we missed her terribly, in addition to saving the money we had been paying her it was a time for our children to learn some important housekeeping skills. This made our last year in Kuching a very busy one but it was fun planning our trip. We used our school time to study about the various places we wanted to go and the sites we planned to see.

Our little school had an extra student from January to June 1973. Harold and Ann Clark, missionaries whom we had met at Glorieta in 1964, had to leave Sabah because of visa difficulties. They came to Kuching to begin another Baptist church. Their daughter, Becky, was Jenny Ruth's age and she requested to study with us rather than at a local school. It was not a lot of trouble to add another child who was studying the same grade as one of ours and she was pleasant company for Jenny Ruth. Often, Ann Clark would cook lunch for us and that made my mornings much easier. In June Becky completed the eighth grade and decided to go to the Singapore American School for her high school years.

As the visa situation in Sabah continued to tighten, all missionaries found themselves having to go elsewhere. Soon Mary and Carl Yarnell also came to Kuching to help in the Baptist work which was beginning to expand in Sarawak. Their daughter, Vivian, was Mark's and Mike's age so it was natural that she came to study with them. Therefore, beginning in September 1973 we again had five students instead of just our own four children. Unfortunately, the Yarnell family left Kuching before that school year was finished because a daughter in the USA had a serious automobile accident and needed their help. Therefore, for the 1974 school year we reverted to just teaching our own children again.

For our curriculum, we followed the course laid out

by the Calvert School located in Baltimore, Maryland. My brothers and I had studied with this same school in China. Calvert School only went through the eighth grade, however, so for Jenny Ruth's ninth grade we ordered materials from the University of Nebraska. This was the same school that I earned my high school diploma from in Taiwan back in 1954. For both schools, the children sent in regular tests which teachers in the USA corrected and returned to them with comments. They all did very well in this learning situation and were ahead in their classes when we returned to America.

****

Mike, Cindy, Mark in Lodge School uniforms – 1971

Jenny Ruth in
St. Mary's Secondary School uniform – 1972

Kuching Baptist Church Charter Members – April 2, 1972

As June 1974 arrived, we were busy preparing to leave Kuching for our second furlough. Charles and Erica Morris came to Kuching to continue the work with the growing Kuching Baptist Church. As we moved out of our mission-owned house, they began moving in. It was hard to leave our Kuching friends but we knew the church would be in good hands. After we left, Chuck and Erica were able to help the church build their own building and call their first national pastor. Due to various government registration difficulties, the church later changed its name to First Baptist Church and continues strong to this day.

We left Kuching on June 15 and flew to Bangkok, Thailand, where we boarded a flight to Europe. Our first stop was Zurich, Switzerland where we stayed a couple of days. Since we were flying on Sabina Airline, a Belgian airline, we then flew on to Brussels. After a day or so there, we arranged to leave our suitcases at the airport and set out on our European tour.

Each of us carried a shoulder bag with three changes of clothes and necessary toiletries. We wore our sweaters/jackets that were necessary for the still chilly weather on the continent. Because our space was so limited, we each chose a small type of souvenir that we could buy from each place we visited. That was when I began collecting souvenir spoons.

Our mode of travel around Europe was the railroad. They have a very good train system and we had purchased Eurail Passes in Singapore that were valid for three weeks. This meant we could ride the trains as often and as far as we wanted to within Europe. Purchasing these passes outside of Europe made the cost very reasonable. Not only did this save us a great deal of money in transportation but also, according to our plans, we spent four nights on the train that saved us four hotel bills. By traveling overnight, we also saved more time for touring during the day. It was a tiring but interesting trip and I am confident our children will never forget it.

We traveled in a circle from Belgium to Holland, Germany, Austria, Italy, Spain, France, and then back to Belgium. After reclaiming our suitcases, we boarded the plane for New York where my dad met us. It was great to see him again and we piled into his car for some more touring. Besides seeing something of New York City, we also drove north and visited various sights in Connecticut and Massachusetts.

Some of the places we saw were historical, like Plymouth Rock, but others were connected to our family history as Dr. Lord and his first two wives were from New York State. It was a meaningful time.

Finally, we headed for Annapolis, Maryland, to see the Bausum relatives. Then it was on to Georgia for an Evans family reunion. At last, we made our way to Campbellsville, Kentucky, where we had booked another missionary house. This one came with the added responsibility of Missionary-in-Residence for Campbellsville Baptist College. For Bob, this also meant being Baptist Student Union Director, as the previous one had just left. He enjoyed having an office on campus (with a secretary) and having daily contact with the students and faculty.

Our house was right across the street from the campus and that was convenient for Bob. Although it was a very small house, with only one bathroom, it met our needs for that furlough. It was too small, however, for my dad to live with us so he rented a married students' apartment just down the street that was very convenient. It gave him his own space but he could take all his meals with us and still feel a part of our family. He also traveled a good bit during that time.

The previous year, Dad's picture had appeared in the Girls Auxiliary (GA) magazine "Discovery," along with pictures of several other retired missionaries. The girls were encouraged to write letters to these missionaries and they did. I think my dad received about 1,000 such letters and he answered each one personally. Many of the girls then wrote him back and a correspondence was established. They would share what they were doing and he would tell them about China and give advice and encouragement in their spiritual growth.

After a while, he had so many of these young friends around the country that he planned a trip to visit some of them. The girls' families and churches welcomed him warmly and he spoke to them about missions. He continued this unique ministry for another few years making a number of trips around the USA wherever he had these GA contacts. Some of the girls and their families became close friends whom he continued to correspond with and visit even to the day of his death.

Our time in Campbellsville was good. The children rode a school bus to school - a new experience for them. We joined the Campbellsville Baptist Church where they enjoyed many activities that our little Kuching Baptist Church could not provide. We all made friends and generally enjoyed our time there. Our children were able to take piano lessons from someone besides their mother, which was another breath of fresh air for them.

We were farther from Georgia, however, so did not get to see Bob's family as often. His mother did come to visit us one time for about two weeks, riding the bus all the way from Rome, Georgia, to Elizabethtown, Kentucky, where we met her. It was a long, tiring trip for her but we were so happy to have her come.

Bob's dad became very ill during this furlough and it was obvious that he would not live much longer. What a blessing that we were still in the USA and Bob was able to visit with him some before the Lord took him Home! It was good for Bob's whole family to be together at this difficult time in their lives.

For Thanksgiving 1974, my brother George and his

family all came to celebrate with us. That little house was bursting at the seams as we slept and fed 15 people for a couple of days, but what fun we had!

****

After having two normal terms on the mission field, things were about to become abnormal. We had prayed much about where we should serve after our time in Kuching and had felt the Lord's leading to go over into West Malaysia. The Mission had invited us to move to the capital, Kuala Lumpur, and begin a new work in the Damansara area where someone had donated a piece of property for a Baptist Church. It sounded like an ideal situation and, to top it off, that was where the International School was located.

It seemed perfect, but we were never able to get government permission to enter Malaysia again. They were already cracking down on the number of foreigners entering their country. After several applications were refused, it appeared that we had no place to return to so the FMB extended our furlough until a visa could be obtained. Fortunately, the Campbellsville College missionary house was still available so we were able to continue our lives as we had for that furlough year.

It was during this time of waiting that the amazing news came about the possibility of Baptists entering the little country of Brunei Darussalam. On that 1966 survey trip when Bob had felt a strong pull towards Kuching, Sarawak, he had also been impressed with Brunei Darussalam and felt a desire to serve there one day. Previously, Baptists had tried to enter but the government turned them down. Now it seemed the time was right.

Immediately we told the FMB we were interested and began to investigate how this could become a reality. Missionaries in Hong Kong said it would be easier to obtain a visa from Hong Kong as Brunei Darussalam was still a British protectorate. Therefore, we packed up, said our good-byes and headed for Hong Kong believing we would have a Brunei Darussalam visa within a few weeks.

It was difficult for our children to make this move. For one thing, our extended furlough had taken us through the end of 1975 and into January 1976. A new school year had already begun and they were all settled into that situation. Our move meant that once again we had to order corre-spondence course materials, as we did not know how long it would be before we could enroll them in a school some-where on the mission field. Jenny Ruth was now in the elev-enth grade and it was the most difficult for her. She hoped that we would settle down soon so that she could enter the Singapore American School and live in our Baptist Hostel there. Unfortunately, there were more delays yet to come.

It was hard to leave Campbellsville and the good friends we had made there. After telling my dad goodbye, we trav-eled to Georgia to see the Evans family once more. Then after a stopover in California to see our friends in Milpitas, we headed towards Asia with a planned stopover in Anchorage, Alaska.

We had been corresponding for some time with a friend in Alaska and received a royal welcome from Baptists in Anchorage. There was snow on the ground and the chil-dren enjoyed playing in that one last time before heading for the tropics again. The home we stayed in had an ador-able dog that we all enjoyed. However, he got in trouble because of us.

Someone in California had made a batch of fudge and divinity candy for our children to enjoy on the long flight to Asia. The candy was carefully packed in our suitcases since we were saving it for that trip. On our return home from church services on Sunday we discovered that the little dog had gotten into our suitcases and eaten the entire batch of fudge. Of course, the next thing he did was to wander around the house, no doubt in misery, throwing up the fudge at various locations. Our dear hostess was so aghast at what her dog had done that after cleaning up her house she stayed up until two in the morning making another batch of fudge for our children to enjoy on the airplane.

From Alaska, we flew around the Arctic Circle visiting Seoul, Korea, and Taiwan on the way. Friends and missionaries in both these places treated us royally and it was a blessed trip. I had not been back to Taiwan since leaving for college in 1954 so was grateful I could meet up with some of my old friends during our short stopover.

Finally, we arrived in Hong Kong where the Mission put us in the YMCA in downtown Kowloon City. Application was made for our Brunei Darussalam visa and we waited. Six of us were crowded into one hotel room that first week. Then even though we were upgraded to two rooms the second week it was an extremely difficult time. We had school lessons in the morning but then there was little to do except walk around town seeing the shops.

After living there several weeks, we decided to take a train ride up to the border of China. When we got out of the city, Mike exclaimed, "So they DO have grass in Hong Kong!" We had been living in a concrete jungle.

Weeks dragged by with no word about our visa. Someone from Brunei Darussalam came for a visit and we were encouraged but still nothing happened. We joined the Kowloon Baptist Church and their various activities helped some with our boredom. Then the Hong Kong Mission gave us one of their houses to live in while we waited. That gave us more space and we settled down to studying each day. Still we were all practically climbing the walls. We decided to buy a piano as Jenny Ruth, especially, had missed having one to play daily.

The damp cold winter months passed and the hot stifling

summer appeared. Our Singapore-Malaysia Mission wrote and suggested we come for the annual Mission Meeting in August. Our hopes for getting into Brunei Darussalam were fading, so this would provide us with a look at any other possibilities for a place of service. We packed up our belongings and left them in Hong Kong trusting we would NOT be returning and flew to Malaysia. How wonderful it was to see all of the missionary aunts, uncles, and cousins, and to cool our hot bodies in the waters at Golden Sands. It was ten days of pure joy.

At that meeting, the missionaries were talking about new directions that were beginning through the Baptist work in Singapore. It seemed that we might find a place of service with their Urban Evangelism Program (UEP) and our children could enroll at the Singapore American School. There was just one problem. The missionaries had discovered that it was easier to apply for a replacement visa than for a brand new visa. Stockwell and Darlyne Sears were currently serving in Singapore but had applied for a visa for Penang, Malaysia to teach at the Baptist Seminary. As soon as they received a visa to Malaysia, they would leave Singapore and then we could apply to replace them to work in Singapore. Thus we began another waiting game.

Time for a new school year arrived, with us still unsettled. It had always been our hope that we would never have to place any of our children in a boarding school, as we believed college was early enough for them to be out on their own. However, at this point we had no choice. It was Jenny Ruth's senior year in high school and Cindy was a sophomore so we decided to place both girls in the Baptist hostel in Singapore and enroll them in the Singapore American School.

Mark and Mike were too young for the hostel, which was only for ninth grade and up, so we kept them with us and continued home schooling them. We stayed in Singapore for a while but when the Sears were able to move to Malaysia and we applied for a visa to Singapore we could not stay in the country as visitors. So the four of us entered Malaysia as tourists and began what we hoped would not be a long wait.

We spent the first three weeks at our Mission's bungalow, Jenderata, in Cameron Highlands, which was a pleasant place to be "stuck." It is cooler in the Highlands so once our lessons were over for the day Mark, Mike and Bob would go hiking or engage in other outdoor activities.

Tea was growing right outside our window so we went on a field trip to tour the Boh Tea Factory. Overall, it was a pleasant stay. Our girls got a long weekend break at Thanksgiving time so they came to be with us. Harold and Ann Clark, their daughter Becky, and Bob and Marge Wakefield also came. It was a memorable experience especially because Harold passed away three months later.

When they all went back to Singapore, we had to leave Cameron Highlands because other people had booked the bungalow for their vacations. We lived in Penang with the Jack Shelby family for the next month. Although they were a family of five, they made room for the four of us to stay in an extra room that had once been a garage. It was crowded for us and for them but we are still friends to this day!

At Christmas time, our girls had two weeks of vacation and they came to Penang to spend it with us. The Baptist Seminary is located in Penang and, since the students were on vacation, we moved into one of the dormitories for that period. Friends lent us their decorations and we managed to make it seem somewhat "Christmassy." Although the situation was less than ideal, we were glad to be together again as a family.

The girls returned to Singapore in January and we moved into a government rest house to continue our wait. Finally, on January 17, 1977, our visa to Singapore was granted and we quickly moved into a mission house there. Not only did we take the Sears' visa slot, we also moved into the house they had just vacated - #1 Butterfly Avenue. It was a comfortable three-bedroom house with an attached study.

We moved in with only the things we had with us in Penang. Our household goods that had been stored in Sarawak arrived next and then our shipment from Hong Kong. Finally, our freight from the USA came and we had all our belongings under one roof again. Our girls moved out of the hostel and back into our home. It was great to have all of our family in the same house again. It had been a long fourteen months!

****

Unpacking and setting up housekeeping became a drawn-out affair because of several factors. First, we had to receive and unpack three different shipments that arrived over a period of several weeks. Secondly, we had already become involved in the UEP ministry even while roaming around Malaysia waiting for our visa.

A fellow missionary, Ralph Neighbour, had worked with two Singaporean young men in writing the correspondence course which we were to direct and we were asked to help in the editing of that material. Therefore, as our shipments of freight arrived, we unpacked the essentials and left many boxes unopened for months. I can still see myself sitting there at the typewriter working on the manuscript while unopened boxes were stacked against the living room wall. After that experience, I promised myself never to move like that again. Unpacking and settling-in must be a priority before getting involved in work.

We immediately enrolled Mark and Mike in the eighth grade of the Singapore American School (SAS) and they did fine finishing out the year they had begun in home schooling. The girls were already well into the school year and their biggest adjustment was going to school from a different location. Our house was located quite far from the school, and the high school and middle school were on two different campuses. Fortunately, SAS ran school buses and the children were able to ride to and from school without much problem. They just had to leave very early in the morning!

With the children settled in school, our possessions all together, and Bob and I involved in the Successful Living Correspondence Course (SLCC), we began to feel that we were at last where we should be. Then in March, a telegram arrived. Our visa to Brunei Darussalam had been granted! We were in a state of shock. It had been more than a year since we had left Kentucky headed for Hong Kong expecting to be in Brunei Darussalam within a few weeks. Our children's lives had been uprooted, our family separated, and now we were finally together recreating some form of stability for us all. If we took up the visa to Brunei Darussalam now it would mean leaving all of our children in Singapore as well as dropping our responsibilities with the SLCC when we were just getting started. We thought God had finally opened a door of ministry for us in Singapore, but what should we do now?

We discussed this with fellow missionaries, communicated with our FMB Area Director, and prayed seeking the Lord's will. Then Bob made a trip to Brunei Darussalam to discuss the situation with the members of the Bethel Mission of Borneo. In the end, we decided that we should not leave Singapore after just settling down. At the same time, we did not want to lose the valuable permission to enter Brunei Darussalam on a missionary visa.

The Brunei Darussalam folks and our Mission finally agreed that Bob would take up the Brunei Darussalam visa while continuing to live in Singapore. Each month he would spend ten days in Brunei Darussalam pastoring those two churches, and the remaining twenty days in Singapore directing the SLCC. I would have more responsibility while he was away since we were co-directors, but the work could continue.

This decision also granted our children a stable home and school life for the remainder of their high school years. Unfortunately for Jenny Ruth, her high school years were just about to end. She would graduate in three months and return to the USA for college. Our time of wandering had negatively affected her the most as she had been in a different school situation for each year of her high school experience. We could only pray that this would not destabilize her for life!

June arrived all too quickly and Jenny Ruth graduated. It was an exciting day for all of us but also an awesome time as we prepared to let our first "bird" fly out of the nest. We celebrated her birthday early and she left Singapore in early August. Her first stop was London, England, where she toured awhile on her own. Then she flew on to the USA and visited in Maryland and Georgia with our families. From there she traveled on to Arkadelphia, Arkansas, and began her studies in piano at Ouachita Baptist University.

Jenny Ruth's good grades in high school allowed her some financial assistance and the school also offered her a work scholarship. Along with the Southern Baptist Margaret Fund for missionary children, she was able, barely, to make ends meet. We were very proud of the way she handled herself and her finances.

Back in Singapore, our remaining three children were all in high school now. Cindy still had two good years to feel settled in her school situation and the boys could look forward to all four years of high school in one location.

Our three remaining children were anxious to have a dog again, so we went to the SPCA and chose a puppy. Before we could bring her home, however, there were two requirements. They had to send someone to our home to be sure we had a safe place to raise a dog and we had to pre-pay to have her spayed. Finally our adorable little puppy could be with us and, when she was old enough, we received a registered letter informing us of the date and time scheduled for her surgery. We named her Tootsie, after the Tootsie Roll candy, and she became a sweet addition to our family.

Work with the SLCC was progressing well. Bob was mostly involved in administrative activities such as arranging advertising and local Baptist support and participation. I enjoyed spending my time answering questions that the students asked when they returned their lessons for checking. Occasionally, we arranged a student get-together and were able to actually meet some of them and share the Gospel face-to-face. It was always rewarding when a student returned to Christ or accepted Him for the first time whether in these gatherings or sharing it with us through the mail.

Our years with the SLCC were happy and productive. Bob and I again joined the Mandarin-speaking Singapore Baptist Church (SBC) but our children joined the English-speaking International Baptist Church. They became very involved in the youth ministry there while we were able to participate fully in our church. Bob still preached in many other churches around Singapore and was gone two Sundays each month to Brunei Darussalam, but I taught a Sunday School class regularly and attended SBC's various meetings.

On occasion, I would join Bob on one of his trips to Brunei Darussalam and, a few times, the children went with us during school holidays. For the most part, however, that ministry was his and it was a blessed one for him. He related to the two Bethel Churches in Brunei Darussalam, one located in the capital city of Bandar Seri Begawan and the other in the little oil rich town of Seria. They were about 60 miles apart. By staying in Brunei Darussalam for ten days he was able to spend one Sunday in each church and have the week in between for various meetings, counseling, teaching, and fellowship.

He developed strong, lasting relationships with the

faithful Christians in Brunei Darussalam and was meeting real needs as neither church had a local pastor at that time. Our lives were very busy with family, school, SLCC and church life. We were daily grateful to finally be settled and serving the Lord through regular ongoing ministries.

****

Jenny Ruth came home for a visit the summer of 1978. The FMB had recently started allowing MKs to make one return visit to their families on the field at Board expense. This was a wonderful provision. After being gone for one year, it helped Jenny Ruth to reunite with her family and to put her life on the mission field in perspective as she went back to the USA and her future there.

In December the Billy Graham Crusade came to Singapore and all five of us sang in the 4,000-voice choir. Participating in that tremendous evangelistic experience was a great blessing!

Cindy entered her senior year and during their interim semester break in January 1979, she made the trip of a lifetime. She had saved her money and we helped, also, so she could join a group of teachers and students making a three-week trip to China. Since this happened shortly after President Nixon had visited China, it was a unique time to visit. The influence of Communism was still very evident in the manner and dress of the people.

Probably the highlight of her trip was to visit Kweilin, where I was born, and try to locate places that would have been there when I was a child. At that time the Kweilin Baptist Church building was being used as a factory for printing on plastic bags. (Later the government returned the building to Christians for its intended purpose.) Cindy and another MK, Martha Ragan, through the help of their tour guide were able to tour the building and at least see something of what it looked like. She took many good pictures on that trip and looked forward to showing them to my dad when we returned to the States.

By this time, the FMB began allowing some flexibility in furloughs and we decided to take a mini-furlough to coincide with Cindy's return to the USA for college. It had been very difficult to send Jenny Ruth back alone but we had no other choice at that point in time. By 1979, we had been back on the mission field long enough to take a three-month furlough so we planned it for the summer right after Cindy's high school graduation. That made her departure from our family circle somewhat easier, although separation from our precious children was always painful.

Cindy graduated in early June and we left the next morning for the USA. That trip was a memorable one. We had booked a hotel in Honolulu, Hawaii, and planned to visit there a few days before traveling on to the mainland. From Singapore, we flew to Hong Kong and then boarded a Singapore Airlines flight to Hawaii.

A few hours before we reached Hawaii our pilot received word that if he landed on USA soil he could not take off again. This was because there had been several recent plane crashes involving the DC10 airplane and the US government had decided to ground all of those planes until the cause could be established. Since that was the type of plane we were on and if we landed on US soil it would be subject to US laws, Singapore Airlines decided NOT to be caught in that situation. Our pilot was told to divert his flight plan, turn around, and fly to Taiwan. We re-crossed the Pacific Ocean flying non-stop from Hong Kong to Hawaii to Taiwan.

We arrived in the early morning hours only to find the Taipei airport closed. Personnel were rousted from their beds and our planeload of passengers was finally processed. Since none of us had visas to set foot on Taiwan soil, immigration simply took all of our passports, put them in a large bag and promised to return them upon our departure. Then we went to a local hotel for a few hours of rest.

By nine o'clock the next morning, we were on our way back to the airport where we were finally able to board a flight that took us to Tokyo, Japan. Again, we went to an airline-provided hotel room for some rest and a shower before returning to that airport to wait for the next leg of our journey. After much confusion and standing in various lines, we were finally able to board a flight that took us to San Francisco.

Our friend, Ralph Adams, had come to meet us in San Francisco the day before and now returned to the airport to get us and take us to their home where we collapsed. Our baggage, meanwhile, had somehow traveled to Osaka, Japan, so it was another day or two before we had any clean clothes to change into or gifts to give our patient friends.

After visiting in California for a few days, we flew on to Texas where we visited with family and attended the Southern Baptist Convention in Houston. Then it was on to Georgia to see Bob's family and meet up with our dear Jenny Ruth once more. What a wonderful reunion!

We had once again booked the Parker Memorial Baptist Church missionary house in Anniston, Alabama (although it was a different house this time), and soon settled in to our summer home. For the July 4th holidays we returned to Rome, Georgia, as Bob's family has an annual get-together at that time.

My dad was on his way from Maryland to stay with us in Alabama for the summer, visiting some of his G.A. friends along the way. He called us the morning of July 5 to chat a few moments and to get directions to Bob's brother's house in Atlanta. Fortunately, Bob and I both talked with him for a few minutes as that was the last time we were to have that privilege.

We returned to Anniston and in the late afternoon received

a phone call telling us that my dad had been in an automobile accident. He had been taken to the hospital in Spartanburg, South Carolina, but was not expected to live. We quickly contacted a neighbor, Marge Sprayberry, who was a fellow church member and she agreed to stay with the children and give them any help they needed. Then Bob and I got into the car and headed for South Carolina.

It was a long tension-filled drive as we kept praying and wondering what we would find upon our arrival. When we finally reached the hospital at about midnight, they told us that my dad had already passed away. We were too late for any final words other than those we had had on the phone that morning.

Bob and I stayed at the hospital until my brother George and his wife, Roberta, arrived. We attended to the details of moving my dad's body to Maryland for burial, looked at his wrecked car, and visited the spot where the accident had occurred. As best we could determine he had left the home of some G.A. girls with whom he had been visiting, and within about 30 minutes had the accident.

Apparently, he got confused trying to get on the interstate highway heading to Georgia and went down an exit ramp. After realizing his mistake, he turned around to go back up, cross over the interstate, and use the correct ramp that would put him on the interstate headed west. There was a stop sign but it was quite far from the intersection. After stopping, he must have moved on up the incline to make a left turn but the overpass railing obscured oncoming traffic from his left and he evidently did not see a truck coming. There was no time for the driver to stop and he hit my dad's car full speed on the driver's side.

Dad did not die instantly and ambulance drivers told us he was kind and grateful to them as they ministered to his needs. However, for an 86-year-old man the trauma was too great and he died on the way to the hospital. We were able to meet the truck driver and assure him that we did not hold him accountable. Although we were heart-broken by our loss, we knew that nothing suited my dad's personality better than to "die with his boots on."

We traveled in two cars together with my brother and his wife to Maryland where the rest of the family was gathering. My brother Howard lived in Maryland and came immediately to Annapolis. Most of the Bausum side of our family was still living in Annapolis but some came from other states because "Uncle Robert" had been dear to all their hearts. Some of my cousins from California and Wisconsin "happened" to be on vacation in Annapolis at the time and were able to stay on for the funeral.

Parker Memorial Baptist Church bought air tickets to fly our four children from Alabama to Maryland. My dad had often talked about having a Bausum reunion but never seemed to be able to bring it all together. As we gathered for that sad occasion it was the closest to a reunion as was possible. Almost everyone was there. My dad would have been so pleased!

We buried him on Sunday, July 8. The service was held at the Weems Creek Baptist Church where he was a member. Dr. Baker James Cauthen, Executive Secretary of the Foreign Mission Board, and his wife surprised us by driving from Richmond, Virginia to attend the service. He made some appropriate comments at our request. The children of the church sang "Jesus Loves Me" in Chinese as my dad had taught them in the Children's Church where he served. Several cousins helped with the music. It was a meaningful time for us all. Interment was at the Hillcrest Cemetery beside my mother.

Dr. and Mrs. Cauthen spent some time with our family that afternoon and were able to look at Cindy's pictures from China and affirm that she had indeed seen places where I had walked as a child. We were all saddened that she did not get to show them to her Granddad but were comforted by the time these dear old friends took to share with us in this way.

We spent a few more days in Maryland while my brothers and I sorted through the things my dad had in our Uncle Fred's house where he had been living. Then we sadly left and drove back to Georgia to visit with Bob's family. I will always remember his mother coming out to greet us as we arrived and taking me into her arms. There was nothing to say. We all had loved my dad so much and it was a great shock and loss. However, in retrospect I praise God that we were in the USA at that time and that we had spoken briefly with him the morning of the accident. God's timing is always so perfect.

That summer went quickly. All too soon, it was time to take Cindy down to Belton, Texas, to enter her chosen school, the University of Mary Hardin-Baylor. This was the school my mother had attended many years before but that was not the reason Cindy chose to go there. We got her situated and then took Jenny Ruth back to Ouachita. Next, Bob and the boys left to spend one week in England on their way back to Singapore and I returned to Maryland.

I needed to sort and store my dad's things. Both my brothers had jobs to return to, but I was able to take a few more weeks of leave from our mission work. So I was "elected" to spend time going through and bringing some kind of organization out of all Dad's belongings. My dad had an "office" in an old garage on my Aunt Mildred's farm. It was full of many things and I spent two solid weeks sorting, throwing away, and packing. Then we moved everything to my cousin Frederick's barn and he kindly let us leave it there until our next furlough when we would all have more time to make other provisions for everything.

My dad had many valuable books and curios as well as personal items so it was not a task to complete in a few days. I flew back to Singapore by myself, stopping to visit Jenny

Ruth in Arkansas and Cindy in Texas before joining my three "boys" who had already returned. Mark and Mike were back in school in Singapore for their junior year of high school and our girls were both in college in the USA. Bob and I returned to our responsibilities with the SLCC and Brunei Darussalam.

****

Successful Living Correspondence Course Co-Directors

Tootsie

Mike, Cindy, Jenny Ruth, Mark, Dorothy, Bob – 1977

4,000-Voice Choir, Billy Graham Singapore Crusade - 1978

Mark's and Mike's last two years at home were good ones for them. They played baseball and football and were involved in various school activities. At church, they were leaders in the youth group and enjoyed singing in several musicals that the youth produced. It was great to have Cindy return in the summer of 1980 for her FMB-provided trip home and we had many fun times together before she returned to Texas for her sophomore year at college.

During Mark's and Mike's senior year of high school, they formed a quartet with two other friends and presented a musical program in the International Baptist Church where they were members. We watched them growing up and realized that in no time we would have an empty nest.

While Bob was away in Brunei Darussalam in the fall of 1980, I received a call from his family in Georgia telling me Bob's mother had passed away on October 17. Her health had been failing for some time but one is never really prepared to hear that a parent is gone.

Immediately, I began trying to reach Bob. It was a Sunday morning and I knew that he would be moving around all day. The Lord is good and I was able to catch him before breakfast and share the sad news. It was a most difficult day for him, though, as he had to preach several times and relate in ministry to people all day long. There was little time to grieve until his responsibilities for the day were over.

Before we returned to Malaysia, Bob had told his brothers that he would not try to go back to Georgia for his mother's funeral. His father was already gone and there were four brothers there to take care of everything. As I had done when my own mother died fourteen years earlier, Bob stayed with his commitments in Southeast Asia while his family laid their mother to rest. It was not as easy to make a return trip to the USA on a moment's notice then as it is today.

Bob was still spending ten days each month in Brunei Darussalam and I began to see some difficulties arising in our home with him gone so much. Not only did our teen-aged boys need their dad around but I found our marriage relationship was suffering, also. Without being aware of it, I began to build a wall of protection between us because it was so hard always saying "hello" and "good-bye." When Bob was away, I was the "head" of the house. When he returned he was the "head." Our marriage and our family were always in a state of fluctuation. I was realizing that this could not continue. Either we needed to move to Brunei Darussalam or Bob needed to stop going back and forth.

Coinciding with this was the realization that everything with the SLCC was about to change. The UEP had been going on for about four years and there were those who wanted to shut it down and begin to work in other directions. In fact, there were parts of the program that had probably "run their course" but we did not feel the SLCC was one of them.

We had some disagreements with some of our fellow missionaries over this issue. People were coming to know the Lord through the SLCC and we wanted to see it continue. In conversations with many of the national leaders in the Singapore Baptist Convention, we found that they felt the same. In the end, we reached a compromise. The Mission began gradually to pull out of supporting the SLCC and the Convention picked up the responsibility accordingly. This was also the "handwriting on the wall" for Bob and me - God was moving us on to other ministries.

As 1981 dawned, we were expecting great changes in our lives. Mark and Mike would leave home in the summer while Bob and I felt the Lord leading us to finally make the move to Brunei Darussalam and serve there full time. Dramatic structural changes were taking place in our Mission also, as the Malaysia-Singapore Baptist Mission would divide into two separate Missions following country divisions.

In May, we received word from Jenny Ruth that she was going to be married in August so another adjustment was crowding into our already crisis-filled year. It was a busy time as we handed over the reigns of the SLCC to local leadership, prepared our boys for leaving home, and carried on long-distance discussions with Jenny Ruth about her upcoming marriage.

Bob was already committed to be the main speaker for the annual youth camp of the Bethel churches in Brunei Darussalam in August. There was no way that he could return to the USA for an August wedding so I arranged to go without him.

After graduating in June, Mark was the next bird to fly from our nest. He and a friend left in July traveling through India before going on to the States. Mike left in August and traveled straight to the USA. The day we took Mike to the airport, we returned home and began packing to move to Brunei Darussalam. One week later the movers came, our house was emptied, and we departed from Singapore. Bob flew to Brunei Darussalam but I took a flight to the USA to attend Jenny Ruth's wedding.

Jenny Ruth had graduated from Ouachita in May and was living and working in Arkadelphia. Cindy had come from Texas to room with her and work during that summer vacation. Since Jenny Ruth's wedding was to be in Arkadelphia, that is where I went first. Mark and Mike soon came and we had the whole family together except for Bob.

It was a lovely wedding with Mark and Mike both escorting their sister down the aisle since Bob could not be there to give her away. Cindy was the maid of honor and I was the proud mother of the bride. A school friend performed the ceremony but Bob had put a short message on tape, from father to daughter, and that was played during the service. In this way, our first-born became Mrs. Art Dunham.

After the wedding, I borrowed a car from some friends and had the privilege of taking the other three children to their schools. First, we took Mark to Southwest Baptist

University in Bolivar, Missouri. Then we drove down to Texas returning Cindy to Mary Hardin-Baylor University. This left Mike and me to make the drive back up to Liberty, Missouri, where he was to enter William Jewell College.

Driving away from each campus seeing my children standing there alone watching me leave was one of the hardest things I have ever done in my life. After leaving Mike, I returned to Arkadelphia to see Jenny Ruth and Art briefly and then drove on to Oklahoma to return the car to our friends. They drove me to the airport and I began the long journey back to Singapore by myself.

In Singapore, I picked up our dog, Tootsie, who had been staying with friends, and she and I flew on the same plane to Brunei Darussalam to join Bob in our empty nest.

****

Friends warned us that the empty nest was a difficult period of adjustment in life, but only when we experienced it did we realize how difficult it really is! It took a couple of weeks before we located a house, received our freight from Singapore and settled down. During that time we stayed in one bedroom of the house that the Bethel Church in Bandar Seri Begawan used for its services. By the time we were into our house Tootsie, who had always been an outside dog, had become an indoor dog and was a great help in filling our empty nest although she could never really take the place of our dear children.

Amazingly, in a country as oil-rich as Brunei Darussalam, there were many houses without telephone service and the house we rented was one of those. To contact anyone by telephone we had to find a public phone or go to a friend's house. This was especially difficult with our children 10,000 miles away. We never had the habit of talking often with them by telephone but it was always comforting to have a phone nearby if needed. I remember one of our children really needed to share with us about something but, by the time a message got to us and we were able to find a phone and call back, it was really too late to be of much encouragement.

We had returned to Southeast Asia in February 1977 and had only taken a brief furlough in the summer of 1979. By 1982, we were due a full-length furlough so after living in Brunei Darussalam for only one year we returned to the USA to see our children and get some much-needed rest.

Jenny Ruth and Art had moved to Kansas City, Missouri, so Art could attend the Midwestern Baptist Theological Seminary located there. Mark and Mike were both in Missouri colleges so it seemed logical that we find a missionary house in that state. The First Baptist Church of Clinton, Missouri, had prepared a lovely old, two-story house for missionaries on furlough and we were happy to stay there from November 1982 to October 1983.

Cindy was still down in Texas but she was able to come to Missouri for Thanksgiving and stayed until after Christmas. The other children we saw more frequently. In January 1983, Jenny Ruth and Art made us grandparents with the birth of their first daughter, Christina Rachel (Christy). It was such a blessing to be with them for that wonderful event and to enjoy our first grandchild during the early months of her life.

Cindy graduated from college in May and we were able to attend that memorable occasion. Jenny Ruth and baby Christy also went with us on that trip. We helped Cindy move to Missouri where the rest of the family lived and she was able to get an office job at Midwestern Baptist Theological Seminary. Before we left the States, we helped her settle into her first apartment. Now all four of our children were living in Missouri so as we returned to the mission field that year we were glad they were close to each other.

Several times over the next few years we enjoyed visits from some of our children. Mark came for a surprise visit at

Christmas 1983 and stayed a month. What a fun time we had with him! Then he returned to Missouri and graduated from college in May 1984 - a year early. Mike came for Christmas 1984 and Cindy came in 1985. These visits helped us handle the empty-nest-syndrome better.

Mike graduated from college in May 1985 and I made a surprise trip back to be there for his special day. That trip was the most unusual one I ever took. I flew on Philippine Airlines so went from Brunei Darussalam to Manila first. Upon arrival, I was informed that my USA flight had already departed! It turned out that the travel agent in Brunei Darussalam had made a mistake. Gratefully, the airline put me up in a hotel overnight and got me on the next day's flight but this delay ruined the surprise element of my trip.

Cindy had planned a family get-together for when I arrived to surprise Mike, but when I was delayed she had to explain why there was a change in her plans. Anyway, I finally got there for Mike's graduation and had a good visit with all the children, even getting to attend Art's seminary graduation as well. (Mark had graduated from college the year before but did not want to "make a big deal" of it so neither of us had tried to come for that.)

After visiting with all our children I began my journey back to Asia, stopping over in New Mexico to visit Mike who was working at Glorieta for the summer. Then I headed for San Francisco and my journey home. However, again there was a mix-up. Unable to confirm my return flight during my six weeks in the USA, I had gone to San Francisco on faith that I could get a seat on the plane anyway. I prayed for a seat - even in the tail of the plane. In the end, the only available seat was in first class! I had to make a quick decision whether to pay $600 extra for that seat or wait indefinitely for another flight. I decided it was worth it to get on home to Bob since I had already been gone for six weeks.

When I tried to pay the extra money, however, my credit

card was maxed-out. The airline would not take a personal check so it looked like all was lost. God was looking out for me, though. Two of my cousins just happened to be at the airport seeing someone off to Europe. Cousin Florence used her credit card to buy my ticket and I wrote her a check for the amount due. Quickly, I told them good-bye and ran to catch the plane that was leaving in 20 minutes!

What a ride back that was! My seat also included a bed so I slept most of the way. When I arrived back in Brunei Darussalam, I thought Bob would be so glad to see me but a friend met me instead, saying that Bob was out of the country! I was glad to be home anyway and I believe Bob was glad to see me later even after I told him how much extra it cost.

Mike lived in France for a year after his graduation from college. On his way back to the USA, he visited us for a month. When he returned to America, he went to live with Mark who had recently moved to Abilene, Texas. During this time Jenny Ruth, Art, and Christy had moved to Indiana and then to California, so it was a time of adjustment for each member of our family.

****

Life was busy in Brunei Darussalam. At first we lived in the capital city Bandar Seri Begawan (BSB) but as Bob had been doing for the past four years we still traveled back and forth to Seria. We continued serving in both of the Bethel Mission of Borneo churches. Bob taught Theological Education by Extension (TEE) both in Brunei Darussalam and over in neighboring Sabah, Malaysia. I was happy to teach Sunday School, play the piano, and be involved in the various church activities as a pastor's wife. Since both churches used English and Mandarin, we were able to continue improving our Mandarin language skills. Except for missing our children, we loved living in Brunei Darussalam because it was a peaceful place and life was not as hectic as it had been in a big city like Singapore.

During this time, travel was an integral part of our lives. Almost every weekend we would pack our bags and drive the sixty miles to Seria to stay Friday and Saturday nights. Bob would teach TEE on Friday nights, we would be involved with various other activities on Saturday and then be in the Sunday morning services. Often Bob would preach for the Korean service that met on Sunday afternoon and then we would return to BSB in time for their service on Sunday evening. Thus, we were in BSB from Sunday evening through Friday afternoon and in Seria from Friday afternoon through Sunday afternoon. It seemed like we were always coming or going. When Bob made a trip over to Sabah, I would simply stay in BSB unless there was some special reason for me to drive down to Seria.

Also once a month we went by speedboat down the river to a tiny town called Limbang in Sarawak. Bob led a Bible Study there and a small group of regular attendees gathered whenever he was able to make the trip. Even though this work was later taken over by the Piasau Baptist Church in Miri, it did not survive. We were always saddened when an outreach did not grow into a strong church, but we had to accept the fact that this sometimes happens.

In 1983, a national pastor began to serve in the Seria Bethel Church and we put more of our energies into serving in BSB. During this time, the BSB church chairman began to move away from some Baptist doctrines and divisions arose in the membership. This was such a problem that the future of that group became uncertain. We spent much time in prayer and in counseling. A crucial turning point came when it was time to elect a chairman for the next year. I was on the nominating committee as was the wife of the current chairman. The outcome was questionable. I remember the

Lord spoke to me one day and assured me that in His time He would work out everything.

When we met to nominate the next year's leaders, even the wife of the current chairman was in favor of another name and we unanimously nominated the person I had hoped for. He was elected by the church, the former chairman decided to join another church, and things began to grow once more in the BSB Bethel Church.

Besides our ministries in Brunei Darussalam, Bob taught TEE in Sabah and was involved in planting a Baptist church in Kota Kinabalu (KK), the capital of Sabah. Although there was already the Likas Baptist Church in KK, the city was large enough and there were significant doctrinal differences so that it needed a second Baptist church. There were strong lay leaders who led in this work but Bob gave the pastoral guidance from Brunei Darussalam and during his monthly visits. In 1984, the Kota Kinabalu Baptist Church was organized and we were two of the charter members. It was during our years in Brunei Darussalam that we began to relate more specifically to Baptist churches throughout East Malaysia.

Charles and Erica Morris were then serving as consultants to Baptists in Sarawak and Sabah but they were approaching retirement. Because of our long-standing connection with East Malaysia, it seemed natural that Bob and I would gradually move into that ministry. In 1982, the Morrises planned the first Pastors and Wives Retreat for those serving in East Malaysia. Over the years, these bi-annual retreats became precious times of sharing for those East Malaysian pastors and families who had little opportunity for mutual fellowship otherwise.

When Bob's work pass for Brunei Darussalam was first granted in 1977, he received a two-year pass that was renewed again in 1979. However, in 1980 they began giving him only a one-year pass. Then in 1984, Brunei Darussalam declared her independence from Britain and things began to change more radically. By 1984, it was difficult to renew Bob's work pass and in 1985, they told him he could NOT renew it. Various friends with some standing in the government's eyes questioned this situation.

The officials explained that they would not renew Bob's work pass because he was working in BSB and the original work pass had been for Seria where the mother church is located. They never told us this before and it sounded like a "cop out" so we offered to move down to Seria if they would renew the work pass. We also explained that we were due a furlough in 1986 and would greatly appreciate being able to stay in Brunei Darussalam at least until that time. Amazingly, the immigration officials decided to give us one more year if we left BSB.

It was annoying to have to move but God was good and led us to a very comfortable house in Kuala Belait (KB) - a small town near Seria. We made the move in October 1985 and had everything in order by the time Cindy came for a visit at Christmas time. Although we were no longer able to work openly with the BSB church we did continue to travel there and give encouragement and training to the faithful lay-leaders in the church. By this time, there was a local pastor in Seria and the church did not need our help, so that final year in Brunei Darussalam we lived in KB where we were not really needed, and were unable to live in BSB where the need was great. This created much unwanted stress.

Bob still traveled to Sabah each month but I never was able to find my niche in the Seria church. In retrospect, I suppose it was a good thing because it made us more ready to leave Brunei Darussalam and see where God was to lead us next. We were very sad, however, when we left Brunei Darussalam in November 1986, because we knew we could not return to live in that beautiful, peaceful country again.

****

Bob and Dorothy with first grandchild,
Christina Rachel Dunham - 1983

Dorothy Leading a Bible Study

Dorothy playing the piano for a worship service

Brunei Darussalam Farewell - 1986

Our furlough home from December 1986 to June 1987 was a missionary house provided by the Richardson Heights Baptist Church in Richardson, Texas. First, we flew to Kansas City as Cindy had decided to leave Missouri and return to Texas at least while we were there. We helped load all her belongings into a U-Haul truck that Bob drove while Cindy and I followed in her car. Mike had been staying in Abilene with Mark who was doing some graduate work at Hardin-Simmons University. After we settled down in Richardson, Mike came to live with us also. At Christmas time, all the children came. Mark drove over from Abilene and Jenny Ruth's family flew in from California. It was great to be together again for a few days.

Many changes occurred in our family during those next few months. I have often referred to this furlough as a very "moving experience" and it was truly that. We had already moved Cindy from Missouri to Texas. After a brief stay there, she decided to move to California to be near Jenny Ruth so we drove another U-Haul truck to Fresno, California, and helped settle her there. Mike decided to move back to Kansas City and look for a job that the Lord graciously provided soon after his arrival. Mark stayed on in Abilene until school was out and then we helped him move back to Kansas City also.

At that time, we left Texas and went to stay for six weeks in a house provided by the First Baptist Church of Raytown, Missouri. Mark stayed with us while he found a job and located an apartment. Now, with our boys settled in Missouri we stopped in California to visit our girls before returning to Malaysia in July 1987.

Because we could not return to live in Brunei Darussalam, the Lord had led us to spend this next term in the city of Kota Kinabalu (KK), Sabah. Over the years, we had been in and out of KK but it had always appeared to me as a place where I would not want to live. However, the Lord touched my heart during our last months in Brunei Darussalam and gave me a desire to go to KK. It was actually a miracle in another way, as well. During the early 1970's, all of our FMB missionaries had to leave Sabah because of government restrictions. It had been fifteen years since any one of our missionaries had been able to live there and now we were going. It was truly God's timing.

Sabah had a Christian governor at this time so we were able to obtain a work pass to live in that state. KK was the best place to live because it was convenient for travel throughout East Malaysia. Now that the Morrises had retired, we were officially liaisons between the FMB and the East Malaysia and Brunei Darussalam churches. This term we would spend a great deal of time flying in and out of KK as we related to all these groups.

Our pattern was to make our home in KK and then travel periodically to the other Baptist churches in Sabah and Sarawak as well as the two Bethel Churches in Brunei Darussalam. We would make at least an annual visit to each church, giving whatever training they might wish and having fellowship with the pastors and leaders. Bob traveled without me at other times for various committee meetings and training that did not require my presence. With our children all gone from home, I enjoyed being involved together with Bob in this varied ministry. Because I am by nature a homebody, I have always given the Lord credit that I could travel so much and find joy in doing it.

Since we were already members of the Kota Kinabalu Baptist Church (KKBC), it was natural for us to worship there whenever we were in town and to be involved with that church as much as our travel schedule allowed. Unfortunately, however, the leaders of that church somehow had the idea that our moving to KK was to become their pastor. When they realized we would be gone a good bit of the time they were not too pleased. Whenever we were in town, we served among them as pastor and wife. Bob preached, I taught a

Sunday School class, we led an English choir, and served on various committees.

It was at this point that I got into trouble with some of the "powers that be." Once again, I was asked to serve on the Nominating Committee with the intent that I would have some new ideas. However, it was the putting forth of such ideas which caused difficulties. Within the committee, we talked about doing things differently and it would seem that everyone agreed. The next day, we would begin to hear gossip that what we had discussed in the privacy of the committee was displeasing to certain people.

In the end, the church voted in many of the new plans and a new church chairman was elected, but a permanent rift was caused between certain members and me. They saw me as the instigator of anything done differently from the past. This made me sad because it was never my intention to cause problems but in the long run the church was better off by moving in some new directions.

Although the FMB discouraged missionaries from pastoring local churches, during 1990, they gave Bob permission to pastor KKBC for a six-month period while they constructed their first church building. This turned into a trying experience for Bob. Outwardly everyone seemed pleased to have Bob pastoring but there continued to be an undercurrent of "we've never done it that way before." This almost destroyed the long-standing relationship he had with the leaders but, praise the Lord to this day we are all still friends!

While we were living in KK we were involved in another outreach point. Once a month we would fly or travel by boat to the island of Labuan, just off the coast of Sabah. There we helped begin the Labuan Baptist Chapel where the Gospel was shared and several people came to know the Lord. After a few years, however, members of the group gradually moved away and the chapel was closed.

****

Before we left the USA in 1987, Jenny Ruth and Art informed us that they were expecting again so I made plans to return the next March to help when the new baby came. In January 1988, however, Mark called to tell us he and Gloria were planning to be married and he wanted his dad to perform the ceremony. So we agreed on an early March wedding and then we would both stop in California to welcome the new grandbaby.

Of course, the best-laid plans often do not work out as planned. On February 24, just a few days before we were to leave Sabah, Art called to tell us that Katrina Ruth (Katy) had decided to come a month early. It was impossible for us to get there immediately and Mark's wedding date was set so we had to settle with visiting them after the wedding as originally planned. Fortunately, some of their church members were able to give much-needed help and, Aunt Cindy and Art's mother were nearby too.

We left Sabah on the last day of February and flew straight to Kansas City. That gave us just a few days to prepare for the wedding that was on March 5. We stayed around for a while longer and then Bob had to return to Sabah. He stopped over in Fresno to meet Katy and spend a few days with the family. I went a bit later and stayed longer, making my total time in the USA exactly one month whereas Bob was only able to stay for two weeks.

Later that year, when Ryan Thomas was born, we were not able to return to the USA, but since his other grandparents lived in Independence we knew that Mark and Gloria would have help from her family. Brittney Rae was born three years later to Mark and Gloria and, again, we were not able to be present for her birth because we were coming on furlough just a few months later.

It is always true for a missionary family that we have

to choose which family events we can return to the USA for and which ones we have to miss. Over the course of our career, we were on the mission field when both of our mothers died although we were in the USA for the death of both of our fathers. We did not get to attend Jenny Ruth's or Mark's graduation from college but were able to be there for Cindy's and Mike's special days. I attended Jenny Ruth and Art's wedding, although Bob was not able to because of a prior commitment, but we were both able to be there for Mark's and Mike's weddings and Bob was the minister who married each of them.

We each made some trips back for special times when it seemed our children needed their parents' help for a while, but these could not make up for the many everyday times when we would like to have been near enough to just drop in for a visit. During the four years we lived in KK, it was a blessing to have Cindy visit us one Christmas but the other children never came to that home. Such is the sacrifice made by missionaries and their children!

One of our greatest joys while living in KK was to be able to get away for a day or two, periodically, and drive up to the Kinabalu National Park. We always stayed in the Perkasa Hotel that looks out on Mt. Kinabalu - the highest mountain in Southeast Asia. In my opinion, it is the most beautiful place in Malaysia. Sometimes we went there with church groups for retreats but the most memorable times were when just the two of us were able to get away for some much-needed quiet together time. Because of our travels, we were often with other people day and night so these special second honeymoons stand out in my memory. Each visit to "my mountain" was a spiritual renewal time because God always seemed so near as we gazed upon such a tremendous creation of His.

Bob was able to make the climb up Mount Kinabalu three times. In 1982, Mark and Mike had come home for the summer and one of their planned activities was a hike up this mountain. Unfortunately, they were not able to make it to the top. The weather was cold and rainy and the wind blew so strongly that their guide would not allow them to make the final ascent beyond 11,000 feet. That was a disappointment but at least they had the experience of trying - one which they will not soon forget.

While we were living in Sabah, Bob climbed the mountain again this time with a group of Christians from the Chinese Section of Likas Baptist Church. They did make it to the top, although the sun was not shining, but Bob did not realize that there is a book at the top where you can sign your name. Therefore, in 1993 he made his third climb, this time with Mark and Gloria while I babysat Ryan and Brittney at the Perkasa Hotel. The weather was beautiful, they saw a lovely sunrise, and Bob remembered to sign his name in the book on the summit. He received a beautiful certificate saying that he made it to the top and it proudly hangs on our bedroom wall today.

By the time we had been in KK for three years, it became evident that the visa situation in Malaysia was tightening. In fact, others living in West Malaysia had already been denied visas and many of our FMB folks had left Malaysia and gone to other countries. Sabah began relating more closely to the West Malaysian government and so the effects of this visa situation began to have influence in the East too.

When we applied for our annual visa renewal in 1990, there was no reply. As long as an application was in, we could stay in the country until it was either granted or denied so, for that next year we actually lived there without a visa. In fact, they never replied to our application and we left Sabah in 1991 for our sixth furlough.

****

Bob and Dorothy
with Mt. Kinabalu in the background, Sabah, Malaysia

For a long time Bob had been after me to return to the land of my birth. 1991 seemed to be the right time, so we made plans. Over the years we realized that our eldest child, Jenny Ruth, had probably been somewhat slighted as we had less experience in child-rearing and less money when she came along. We invited her to travel to China with us in the summer of 1991. Art graciously agreed to keep Christy and Katy and let Jenny Ruth come on this trip of a lifetime. We met her in Singapore and had a nice visit there first. Then we flew on to Hong Kong for a couple of days before going into the mainland.

Our first stop was Shanghai. We were immediately amazed at the crowds of people. I remembered my mother's words when she first arrived as a new missionary in China, "I never knew what a multitude was until I came to China." We stayed in the famous old Peace Hotel located near The Bund. As we walked around town I took many videos. Bob, meanwhile, would greet the passers-by in Mandarin. After awhile I would turn around to look for him but all I could see was a crowd. When I walked back, there was Bob in the center talking in Mandarin to total strangers. What a delight!

My favorite experience in this huge city was walking in the section called the Old Town. I could imagine my great-grandparents Dr. and Mrs. Lord, and my great-aunt Mary Bausum Barchet, walking these same streets. It was awesome! We tried to locate where Mary and Stephen Barchet were buried but could never solve that mystery.

It was also a blessing to worship in two different churches while in Shanghai - a morning and an evening service. One was a former Methodist church and the other had been a Baptist church. Now they were "Christian" churches. All the open churches in China were either "Christian" or "Catholic" churches. After each service, we had interesting talks with various church leaders and even with pastors who were incarcerated by the Communists in the early days.

We visited the former Shanghai Baptist University and talked with a record keeper there who had known Baptist missionaries living in Shanghai prior to the Communist take-over. The school is still a university but is now government-run.

We left Shanghai by train and rode all day long to reach the city of Ningpo where my great-grandfather, Dr. Lord, had served as a missionary for forty years. That train ride was an interesting experience. We chose to ride a train so that we could see some of the countryside and we did. We saw farms, small towns, and many everyday people doing everyday things.

The ride itself was tiresome but we accomplished our purpose. One unique memory stands out from that ride. There was a large container on the train with boiling hot water in it. Every passenger (except us!) had brought along their own tea leaves in some kind of jar or cup. Most of them carried old Nescafe jars for this purpose. They would fill their jar with the boiling water and have hot tea to drink. Since we had not known about this convenience we had to buy what-ever we needed to drink from passing vendors.

There was a "new" Ningpo where our hotel was located but we spent our time in the "old" Ningpo where the build-ings are over two hundred years old. We KNEW that my forefathers had lived and walked there! I had gathered some information from various books about Hudson Taylor to learn where my great-grandfather might have lived. We booked a taxi for one whole day to drive us around looking for clues. It was a bit like a mystery adventure and our driver quickly got as excited as we were.

With his help and my prior research, we were able to locate the school that Jemima Poppy Bausum had begun when she came to Ningpo. The principal was so pleased to meet us that she called all of the teachers down to the yard and we posed for a picture together. We found a church building, now closed, which I firmly believe Dr. Lord built.

In addition, we were able to visit with the pastor and some leaders in the local Christian Church. It was not Sunday, so we did not get to worship with them, but we learned that Hudson Taylor had been instrumental in beginning this church and his grandson has since been there to preach.

I had brought a picture of my great-grandparents' graves and we showed it to long-time residents. They told us where the cemetery had been but now a housing estate stands on that land. This was a disappointment but we knew that those dear souls were in heaven with God anyway.

At the end of that day, our taxi driver asked if we would like to visit his home. What an honor that was for us! He showed us around a large house that encircled a big open courtyard. His family had owned that entire house before the Communists took over. Then the government had moved in a number of other families so that each family had a room and shared a common kitchen, bath, and the courtyard. This 38-year old man, his father, and a grandmother lived in two adjoining rooms in that former "mansion." He could not remember when it had been otherwise!

We sat in his living room, which was also his grandmother's bedroom. This elderly woman lay there in an ancient inlaid-mother-of-pearl bed that had been her wedding bed. She was ninety-one years old and had bound feet. What a beautiful face she had! Her skin was smooth, not wrinkled, and she had a beautiful smile. We could not talk with her as she spoke only the Ningpo dialect but we used smiles and touches to convey to her our love.

It was a precious unexpected interlude in all of our touring. The driver's father was so hospitable and served us warm cokes, as there was no refrigeration. Throughout the day, our driver had shared with us his dream to leave China and go where he could earn enough money to have the everyday things we take for granted. Our hearts ached for him and we longed to be able to do more than just give him a big tip for the day's kindnesses. It was hard to tell him good-bye.

That evening at our hotel, I kept thinking about one spot we had visited where the battery on our camera went dead and I could get no pictures. I persuaded Bob to call us another taxi in the morning to take us to that one spot again. As before, we booked a taxi through the hotel management.

How surprised we were when our driver from the day before showed up! Not only did he come to take us he refused any pay and even brought us gifts to remember him. I got my pictures but most importantly, we had found a real friend. The Ningpo visit was definitely a trip back in time for us - an unforgettable peek into my ancestors' lives.

From Ningpo we flew to Beijing, the capital of China. We found it generally "colder" than Shanghai in that people were less friendly. Even when we attended a worship service there, the pastor seemed cold and perhaps afraid to be friendly with foreigners. We could understand this as the government, no doubt, had tighter controls in Beijing. We saw many interesting sights including the Great Wall, the Forbidden City, and the Summer Palace. It was interesting and informative but, overall, the place we enjoyed the least.

When we left Beijing, we flew on an old Russian plane down to Kweilin. There are no words to describe the feeling I had as our plane flew in low over those unique mountains rising up in the middle of massive rice paddies. I found it difficult to accept that I was really back in Kweilin. We stayed at the Holiday Inn and they kindly gave us a very nice room with a beautiful view of the city and surrounding mountains. I was up early the next morning taking videos as the sun rose over scenes that had been my childhood world.

I had brought along a map from my dad's book <u>Pass It On</u>, but it was only of the former Baptist compound where we had lived. We did not know how to find that compound. The first morning we set out on foot to locate the Baptist Church. Once again, we found people very friendly and interested in why we had come and what we were looking for.

A man on a bicycle, after learning that we were looking for the former Baptist Church, said he knew where it was and would take us there. He walked his bike with us walking alongside through narrow, crowded streets that felt so familiar to me. When we arrived at the church, he knocked on a side door, explained to someone inside who we were and then went his way while we received a royal welcome.

The church folks were thrilled when they learned who I was and showed us around the building. When Cindy had visited there in 1979 it was a factory, but later the government returned it to the Christians for its intended purpose. As we toured that old stone building built in 1920, I had the feeling that "I've been here before!" It was an awesome experience for me.

Then we asked the folks if they knew where the Baptist compound had been and one of them agreed to take us there. It was now a Medical College and still walled in with a gatekeeper as it had been in my childhood. When we explained that I had been born there, the authorities welcomed us warmly and we freely walked around for a long time using my dad's map to try to determine where all the former buildings had stood.

There was one old building remaining which seemed to be part of the Girls' School where my mother had been the principal. Using the map, I determined where our house probably stood although an American bomb had destroyed it before the Japanese war even ended. Part of the old city wall was still standing behind where I had played as a child and I picked up two stones from there to bring back to George and Howard when we returned to the USA.

Besides walking around the city, we also took a daylong boat ride down the Li River that was very nostalgic for me.

Although the tour boat we rode on was motorized, we still saw houseboats, cormorant fishing birds, and sights that have not changed for centuries. I KNEW I had been on this river before! The scenery along that ride was absolutely gorgeous. I just wanted to keep snapping pictures every minute.

Kweilin is famous for its beautiful mountain formations and for the caves inside those mountains. Since our family had used those caves to hide in during World War II, we took a tour through one cave and did some climbing on some of the mountains. Even though the Japanese destroyed 90% of Kweilin during the war, it still felt like "home" to me and those four days were a never-to-be-forgotten experience. I was SO grateful that Bob had insisted I should return to the land of my birth. It is easy for MKs (missionary kids) to feel as though they have no roots so that visit had special meaning to me.

We had planned a Sunday in Kweilin so that we could worship in the former Baptist Church. How thrilled we were to see the tour guide who helped us get to and from the airport come slipping into the church service to sit beside us. He said he had never been in a Christian church before and wanted to see what it was like. Perhaps officials had sent him there to spy on us; we do not know. All we know is that he heard the Gospel and we pray a seed planted in his heart that day has already born eternal fruit.

The day we left Kweilin to return to Hong Kong two special events occurred. A young man we had met came to our hotel to see us before we left. He brought two friends and they asked us to tell them about Jesus. What a thrill that was and we were grateful to be able to give them a Gospel of John before we bid them good-bye. At the airport as we were leaving, the immigration men were smiling and telling us to, "Come back!" After living in Malaysia with visas so difficult to get and fearing how Communist China would treat us,

I will always remember such welcoming friendliness from government officials in the city of my birth.

****

For our 1991 to 1992 furlough, we had arranged to be missionaries-in-residence for the California Baptist Convention located in Fresno. We recognized that this western state did not have as many furloughing missionaries as the southern states had but there was another reason we were interested in this ministry. Both of our daughters were living in Fresno.

Cindy graciously agreed to let us share her two-bedroom apartment since the convention had no housing for their in-residence program. Because Cindy lived about a five-minute walk from Jenny Ruth's family, it was neat to share many daily experiences with these dear ones. Our boys still lived in Missouri so we made several trips back east to have time with them as well as seeing our brothers and many long-time friends.

Living in California and being near our two grand-daughters gave us the idea of taking them to Disneyland. We had received several invitations to speak in churches in southern California so we planned a ten-day trip with them that included some "work" and some "play." At this time, Christy was nine years old and Katy had just turned four. We were a bit surprised that Katy would go with us on such a long trip but it turned out she was the most excited one in the bunch!

The Wednesday before going to Disneyland we had speaking engagements in two different churches. The girls and I visited the church where my cousin Mary Catherine's son, Paul Krake, was music director. Christy and Katy were very good to sit in the pews while I shared with the congregation about Malaysia. Meanwhile, Bob had driven on to share in another church. When he finished speaking, he returned to pick us up and we headed for our motel, all excited about going to Disneyland the next morning.

As we drove down the Santa Ana Freeway, a careening wheel that had flown off a passing vehicle suddenly struck our car. It hit the side of our car where Katy was sitting and then flew on down the freeway hitting several other cars. We all pulled to the side of the road and assessed the situation. Fortunately, no one was hurt and the car could be repaired.

Of course, there was some delay while we waited on the police to arrive and make their report. Bob was outside talking with the other drivers involved but the girls and I sat in the car and talked about what had happened. Naturally, they were quite shaken up and crying some. To calm them, we began to talk about all the good things we could think of about the accident. Since we had no paper handy we made a mental list. No one was hurt. The car could still be driven. Someone in another car had a cell phone with which to call the police. We had completed our speaking engagements at the churches. The girls were soon involved in helping me make the list and their fears gradually subsided.

Katy, however, was still troubled about something. "Why did that man want to hit us?" she asked. I tried to explain that it was an accident. He did not mean to hit us but his wheel suddenly flew off and there was no way he could stop that. She did not seem convinced. Later, as we were standing around with everyone else the driver came over to us. He was a fine young man just returning from church himself and I asked him to talk with Katy.

Immediately he kneeled down to get on Katy's eye level and gently told her how sorry he was for the accident. After that, she seemed to be fine. By the time we reached our motel, the girls were all right and we all finally got to sleep about midnight.

After two exciting days at Disneyland, we traveled on

further south where Bob and I spoke at a church very near the Mexico border. It was so near that we decided to take a day trip across into that country so the girls could at least say they had been there.

Our next stop was the San Diego Zoo and that was fun. We had arranged for a stopover in Palm Springs in connection with a timeshare presentation. It was a very nice hotel and we had a great time. On that whole trip, four-year-old Katy made much over whether we were staying in a "h"otel or a "m"otel. It was a memorable trip!

Three of my cousins live in California so we had some special times with them on this furlough, too. I especially remember having the privilege of being the guest speaker for a teachers' retreat planned by June Bausum Powers. She would annually take her pre-school teachers on a weekend retreat and it was my special joy to be included in that experience while we lived in California.

Then Bob and I drove on further north to see some of that beautiful state as well as to share about missions in various churches. We spent one unforgettable weekend in a cabin at the foot of Mount Shasta as guests of the area missionary.

That Sunday morning there was an earthquake tremor felt around Mount Shasta. Later we learned that a few days earlier, there had been a strong earthquake in Palm Springs. This second one had also been quite strong in the part of California where I had just been for the teachers' retreat. We praised God that He kept us moving just ahead of the earthquakes. Of course, others suggested that our visiting each of these places might have caused the earth to quake!

Whenever we visited Missouri, we had the precious privilege of getting to know Mark's children better. Ryan was an adorable almost four-year-old and Brittney had her first birthday while we were in the USA. Every moment with them was treasured. We also were able to meet our future daughter-in-law, Mike's fiancée Marilyn. They were planning a June wedding before we returned to Malaysia so Bob could officiate.

As the time drew near for our return to the mission field, we began to wind down things in Fresno. We were able to get a missionary house in Liberty, Missouri, for our final month in the USA. This gave us a "home" during the time of the wedding and some final days with our sons and their families. It turned out that at the last moment Cindy, Jenny Ruth and her family all decided to move from California back to Missouri so we were able to help with that gigantic task. This meant that all four of our children were once again located in Missouri close to each other. I call that a "God thing."

****

That final month in Missouri was a "God thing" in more than one way. We had decided to buy a house in preparation for our retirement. This was something we had often discussed but we had never been interested in having to worry about renting out a house while we were 10,000 miles away. Now everything seemed to come together. Our children were all located in one general area so that seemed a logical place to buy a house. Cindy needed somewhere to live so we arranged for her to live in our house and care for it until we were ready to retire. The plan seemed a good one but we had only one month in which to make it happen.

First, however, was the all-important wedding. Mike and Marilyn were married on June 13, 1992 in Independence, Missouri, in the same church where Mark and Gloria had been married – Immanuel Baptist Church. It was definitely a family affair. Bob officiated. Jenny Ruth played the piano. Mark was the best man. Gloria was the matron of honor. Ryan was the ring bearer. Christy and Katy were flower girls. It was an honor for Cindy to help serve at the reception and I was mother of the groom. It was a memorable occasion for us all.

After Mike and Marilyn left on their honeymoon, we began house hunting. One of the first houses we saw was the one we eventually chose to buy. We made our decision after some brief searching. The hard part was getting all the paperwork done before our departure date. The real estate agent and the banker both leaned over backwards to help make it happen.

When we did the actual closing, Bob had gone to Rome, Georgia, to see his brothers one last time so he was not present to sign the papers. The banker allowed him to sign them upon his return and we stuck them under the loan officer's door as we left for the airport early Monday morning to depart the country!

In addition, no one had informed me that we needed a cashier's check for the down payment so the banker once again used his prerogative and accepted a personal check from me for a hefty amount. The real estate agent continued to marvel at how God had worked to make it all come together within our very brief timeframe. We closed on Saturday morning - another exception the banker made especially for us. Cindy moved her furniture in on Saturday afternoon and we left the country early Monday morning.

We did not fly directly to Malaysia, however. We flew to London and Cindy joined us there for some sightseeing. I took a side trip to Great Yarmouth where my great-grandmother Jemima Poppy Bausum Lord had lived as a child. Bob and Cindy, meanwhile, went to Wales - home of the Evans name. Then we went down to Germany and visited some other places of interest.

That summer of 1992 was extra special for we attended the first reunion between the American Bausums and the German Bausums. We met in Rodheim, Germany, where my great-grandfather John George Bausum had been born. When he left there to become a missionary in Malaya, he left a brother and cousins behind. Now, more than a century later, the descendants of both sides of the family gathered for the first time. Since Germans do not normally have family reunions, as we Americans descended on that small town our German cousins had to explain to the town folk what was happening.

About seventeen of us from the USA were able to attend. Including our German relatives there were more than one hundred who attended some, if not all, of the planned activities. It was an unforgettable weekend. We Americans stayed in our relatives' homes even though most of them spoke little or no English. When we gathered for presentations, one of them translated. We were given a walk-around-town tour of locations relevant to our family. Our cousin Manfred had placed a thirteen-generation family tree on a wall in his courtyard showing the names of all who attended the reunion and our relationship in the family.

On Sunday morning, the American Bausum family "took over" the worship service in the church where John George Bausum had spent his early years. The congregation was mostly the German Bausum family, many of whom do not attend church regularly. Various ones from America led in the music and other parts of the service. As the missionary from the family, they asked me to bring the message. I count that as one of the highest privileges in my lifetime. By God's grace, I tried to tie in something of our family history while sharing the Gospel to those dear people who may never have heard it clearly before. It was a wonderful climax to this first-time Bausum reunion.

The next day Cindy returned to the USA to look for a job and begin to settle down in Missouri, and we flew on to Malaysia. Another furlough was finished and another term of service on the mission field was about to begin.

****

Our house in Independence, Missouri –
Cindy and Jake lived here until we retired

When we left Sabah in 1991, we had already been living there without a visa for one year. It had been our hope to get a visa for Sarawak and finish our career living and serving in that state. However, this was not to be. The government denied our application and there seemed to be no way to change that decision. Thus, when we landed in Singapore in July 1992, we faced the question of where we should live for the next four years.

As we discussed the options with our Area Director and others, it became apparent that the prevailing opinion was for us to take up residence in Johor Bahru (JB), West Malaysia, while still maintaining some kind of relationship with the East Malaysian churches. How this was going to work out was not yet clear.

Soon after our arrival, we went across the causeway from Singapore to JB to look for an apartment and to purchase a car. Our freight came from KK where it had been stored during our furlough and we began to set up housekeeping. After only three weeks there, however, we made our first trip to East Malaysia to re-establish our relationship with those churches. Our hearts were really in East Malaysia, so we needed to determine how we could live in the West and minister in the East at the same time with nine hundred nautical miles separating the two places.

To complicate matters, the FMB asked if we would be willing to go and live in Sri Lanka for two months. It seemed that their government had granted a certain number of visas for Baptist missionaries but, at that time, Baptists lacked one missionary couple to fill their quota. If no one filled the remaining visa slot Baptists would lose it. Therefore, we agreed to go and hold a visa slot for two months until the assigned missionaries were able to arrive. Since we had no visa for Malaysia this was not a problem so we "sort of" moved into JB, greeted our long-time coworkers in East Malaysia, and then left the country.

Living in Sri Lanka was an entirely different world. For a time we stayed in the old Galle Hotel. It was historic, but far from the most comfortable place we have ever stayed. While eating breakfast one morning we heard a loud explosion. Everyone rushed outside to see what had happened. Just a few hundred yards from our hotel a suicide bomber on a motorcycle had run into a military cavalcade killing three or four top men in the Sri Lankan Navy - another reminder that all was not well on this tiny war-torn island.

Later, we moved into an apartment that was located on the Baptist Convention property. Many of the niceties we had in Malaysia did not exist in Sri Lanka. It took a great deal of our time and energy just to live there. We did some language study mostly for fun. Bob had opportunities to preach on a number of occasions but for the most part, we felt rather useless. Our time was limited. Our purpose was to hold a visa so there was not the plan, nor inclination, to become too involved in any ongoing ministry since we would only be leaving soon. We were in Sri Lanka through Christmas 1992 and then returned to Malaysia in early 1993.

Since we had no visa in Malaysia, we began living in JB as what I laughingly called "professional tourists." The Malaysian government had not given any professional visas to missionaries since the late 1980s but continued to give American citizens an automatic three-month tourist visa upon entering the country. That is what we received whenever we entered Malaysia. When the three months expired we would exit the country and then re-enter, receiving another three months. That became our pattern for the next eight years.

Although we were living in West Malaysia, we still served as consultants to the East Malaysian Baptist churches. In this capacity we visited every Baptist church in Sabah and Sarawak at least once a year. We would give training, counseling, and encouragement to the church leaders and members, just as we had done while living in Kota Kinabalu,

Sabah. Bob even helped plant a church in Kuching "in absentia." This was possible because there were strong lay leaders there who carried on the ministry between Bob's visits. Agape Baptist Church continues faithfully, today, even though they have never had a fulltime pastor.

When we were at home in JB we helped in two new church starts outside of JB town but still in the state of Johor. For a while Bob gave assistance to an Indian pastor who was beginning a ministry in Segamat, and we both helped a Chinese pastor with an outreach in Kluang. Gratefully, several people came to know the Lord through these efforts although neither of these works grew strong. Both eventually closed.

Although we enjoyed ministering among the JB churches, we had difficulty finding our niche there because we traveled to East Malaysia several times a year for extended visits. When we were in town we led a few seminars and Bob was always preaching somewhere, often several times on a Sunday. Even I was asked to speak from time to time proving that the JB churches were very hard up for speakers!

However, we never really felt like we "belonged" on the JB scene because we were always in and out of town. In a way, it was a repeat of our life in KK where the KKBC members felt slighted because we were often away in ministry elsewhere. I felt it created a gap which we never really were able to close. We made some good friends and had many meaningful experiences but there were many disappointments too. Looking back, our happiest times were when we were in East Malaysia.

We lived in what I would call a penthouse apartment. It was the top floor of a three-story apartment building but within our apartment there were two floors. It was spacious and comfortable although hardly "fancy." Because we traveled so much, it was a very safe place to be left empty so often and a wonderful hideaway in which to recoup when we came home exhausted from ministry and travels.

Our travels not only took us to the East Malaysian states of Sabah and Sarawak but also to the country of Brunei Darussalam where we had lived before. There as in Malaysia, we were able to go in and out as tourists with an American passport.

We were planning some regular ministry in BSB while their pastor went for nine months of study in England, beginning in September 1996. When we arrived in the BSB airport on November 2, 1996, immigration officials told Bob he could not enter the country. This came as a complete shock to us. We had to re-board the same plane and fly back to Singapore. There, they detained us on the plane until everyone else had disembarked. Then we were escorted to a special immigration desk where they tried to determine if we were "dangerous" or not - perhaps trafficking in drugs.

They soon cleared us but such an event had never happened to us before and it took us some time to process what had occurred. Apparently, the Brunei Darussalam immigration department had finally gotten their files computerized and placed black marks by the name of any "undesirable" they did not want in their country. They considered Bob such a person because he was a Christian pastor. He would no longer be welcome in Brunei Darussalam. That was a very sad day, especially for Bob.

In the months that followed, I made a number of trips into Brunei Darussalam to minister to the folks in what ways I could. I felt it was a great honor for them to accept me and I had some wonderful experiences in teaching, counseling, speaking at camps, etc. When our dear friend John Mathews passed away, and Bob could not enter Brunei Darussalam even for such an occasion, I had the privilege of speaking on behalf of our family at the funeral.

There were two times over the next few years that Bob was able to enter Brunei Darussalam because an immigration agent neglected to run his passport through the computer. However, when it came time for us to say our final farewells, he was turned back at the border and I had to go in alone to enjoy all the dinners and receive all the gifts on behalf of us both. It was a bitter pill to swallow.

****

Bob was on the Board of Management for the Malaysia Baptist Theological Seminary (MBTS) for the last twelve years that we were on the field. In conjunction with this responsibility, he made at least two trips a year to Penang where the seminary is located. He found great joy in serving with this institution that is vital to the training of local pastors and leaders in Malaysian churches.

Two years before we left Malaysia the MBTS and the Malaysia Baptist Convention (MBC) asked us to write a history of Baptists in Malaysia. The International Mission Board (IMB - formerly FMB) granted us permission to let that be our priority for the years 1999 to 2000.

After laying down general plans for what such a book should include, we began traveling all over the country doing interviews. What a wonderful experience that was! We did over 200 interviews with either individuals or groups from the various churches. In doing this, we heard many thrilling testimonies of how God had worked in these dear people's lives. It was challenging to us as well as encouraging.

On May 1, 1999, Satan tried to bring a halt to our interviewing and research by attacking me. It was Saturday night and Bob was attending a service with one of the Indian church groups. I decided to mop the floor while waiting for him to return home as we were expecting guests on Monday.

I can still recall clearly the moment my heel hit that drop of water and my feet went out from under me. By rights, I should have fallen backwards and cracked my head on the hard tile floor but somehow, as I grabbed for something to stop my fall, my body fell forward instead. I felt one leg twisting sideways as I hit the floor and knew I was in trouble. After collecting myself for a few moments, I began to try moving to see what I could or could not move.

At first, I thought all was well but then I realized I could not move one leg without pain. After laying there for about half an hour, I managed to drag myself across the floor without too much pain and reach the telephone. Fortunately, Bob was in town, I knew where he was, he was not preaching that night, and that church building had a telephone. He rushed home as soon as I explained what had happened.

After an ambulance ride to the hospital, it was determined that I had cracked my right hip and the doctor suggested a partial hip replacement given my age. By 1 p.m. on Sunday, I was in surgery. They only kept me in the hospital a few days and then sent me home without any therapy. Because we lived on the third floor, with no elevator, getting up there was quite an adventure that I would not care to repeat.

Once I was safe in our home Bob took good care of me and the Lord blessed me with rapid healing. One of my sweetest memories was when several of Sarawak's tribal home missionaries were in JB on a mission trip and came to visit me. They gathered around me and prayed in the Iban language for my healing. Although I could not understand their words, I could hear the fervor of their prayers and I know the Lord heard! Three weeks later leaning on a walker, I was on the road again with Bob interviewing for the Baptist history.

In our travels, we were welcomed into homes, church guest rooms, and fancy hotels where the bill was paid by thoughtful brothers and sisters in Christ. After I broke my hip, people went out of their way to provide for my needs often coming to our room for the interviews so I would not have to walk up and down stairs so often.

After the interviews, we spent countless hours listening to the tapes and making notes as well as researching whatever documents we could get our hands on for this project. Many pictures were made available to us and everyone we talked with was excitedly looking forward to reading a written up-to-date history of Malaysian Baptists.

After about one year of researching and interviewing, we entered the second year of the project that we had set aside for the actual writing. Someone once told me that "writing is hard work," and he was correct. Writing, re-writing, asking others to proof read and edit, all took much time and energy. There were times when we wanted to quit but the time constraint was on us so we pressed forward. Originally, we had planned to retire when Bob turned 65 but had extended for an extra year in order to complete the history. We did not want to extend another year!

Finally, in June 2000 we had the book ready to go to press. Bob traveled to Kuala Lumpur (KL) for talks with the printer and to deliver some pictures we wanted to include in the book. After that conference, he was asked to meet with the MBC chairman who proceeded to inform him that the book could not be printed. What a blow! The excuse he gave was "for security reasons," but we realized that there were underlying reasons as well.

So as we packed up to leave Malaysia for our final furlough we also packed up all the materials we had gathered in writing the history. We delivered these to the seminary for a database that future historians could use. The manuscript we had written, however, we brought back to the USA with us.

After we had been back in the USA for about two years, the Malaysia Baptist Convention contacted us to say they were ready to print the book. We re-worked some of the manuscript, created an index, and then sent the whole document to Malaysia where it was printed in 2003.

Bob had the privilege of returning to Malaysia that year to be there for the official launching of the Malaysian Baptist History, <u>Great Things He Has Done</u>. The theme for the Convention's annual meeting that year was the book's title and Bob was the main speaker for that 50th anniversary event. By then we were over the disappointment and were just grateful that Baptists in Malaysia were finally able to have their history. God is good and His timing is always perfect!

****

EPILOGUE

*A*fter our children left home to attend college and live in the USA, it was a blessing to have each of them return for various visits. This helped to ease the pain of such long-distance separation.

Each one was able to return at FMB expense the summer after his or her freshman year in college. We greatly appreciated this provision by our Board as it helped our children make the transition from living in a foreign country to living in the USA.

Over the years, Cindy was able to make a number of visits - about every five years. She would save up vacation time from work as well as her money and come for five or six weeks at a time. That was fun!

Besides the FMB-provided visit, Jenny Ruth only came one other time, in 1991 when we took her to China with us. However, in 1994 her daughter, Christy, came and spent the summer with us. That was quite an adventure for an eleven-year old!

Mark made another visit while he was still single and then one more when he brought his family with him in 1993. Mike was able to make two other visits while he was single, one at Christmas 1984 and the other after his yearlong stay in France. Then in 1997, he brought his family, also.

During our years of living in JB, we took one more furlough in the summer of 1995. We again stayed in the missionary house provided by the Second Baptist Church of Liberty, Missouri. Besides the official FMB-provided trips, one or both of us made a number of personal trips back to the USA for various needs/celebrations in our children's lives.

In 1996, I returned to help welcome Mike's and Marilyn's first baby girl, Lindsay Marie. Two years later I came again when Aubrie Lynn was born. Such times were special privileges. Bob and I returned for a month's vacation in 1997 and again in 1999. We were grateful to live in an age when travel was so fast and easy we could keep family ties that close from such a distance. Remembering that my great-grandparents had left their homes as missionaries never to return, I knew we were tremendously blessed.

Finally, in 2000 it was time to leave the mission field and prepare to retire from serving with the FMB/IMB. There is no mandatory retirement age and one never truly retires from serving the Lord but we came to feel it was the right time to move back to our home country and begin to put roots down while we still had our health.

It was hard to say good-bye to all of our Malaysian friends. There were many farewell dinners and we received countless treasured gifts - reminders of friendships established over the years. Teenagers we had known when we first went to Malaysia were grownup and pastoring churches. Their children called us "Grandpa and Grandma." We loved so many dear friends because of shared experiences. It was even hard to leave those with whom we had had some disagreements or misunderstandings.

We sold most of our furniture, gave away many items that others could use, threw away years of gathered junk, and then packed up the rest and shipped it to Missouri. Here in our own house at last, we live among precious memories - kept alive by wall hangings, souvenirs on shelves, and occasional letters from Asia. Mostly these memories are stored in our hearts and one day we will renew and enjoy them for eternity in Heaven. As I look back over not only my own life but also that of my ancestors, I give God all the glory for truly "He Led All the Way!"

Jenny Ruth, Mark, Mike, Cindy – 2005

Dorothy, Bob, Laddie - 2005

APPENDIX

The following is a re-telling,
in more careful detail,
of the story of my ancestors.
I have included some charts
with the hope
that the various relationships
will be made clearer.

A DELIGHTFUL INHERITANCE

*A*s a child, I was embarrassed to tell my middle name, thinking my friends would make fun of me. It was only after I was grown, and understood the story I am about to tell, that I realized how blessed I am to be named **DOROTHY LORD BAUSUM.** My name is a tribute to two outstanding missionary families who remained faithful to God's calling in spite of many difficulties and tragedies.

When I think about my family I stand amazed at how God has blessed me! I did nothing to deserve this but am merely the recipient of a rich heritage.

"O God,
you have given me
the heritage
of those
who fear your name."

Psalm 61:5

Dorothy Lord Bausum Evans
Independence, Missouri
2007

BAUSUM

MALAYA

*M*y great-grandfather, **John George Bausum**, was born on June 8, 1812, in Rodheim, Germany. He received baptism in the state Lutheran Church as a baby and I saw the written record of this event in 1992 when we visited Rodheim. Although the State church in Germany is not evangelistic, somehow John George came to know the Lord Jesus personally. Perhaps that was why he left Germany and went to England where I assume he did some theological or Biblical studies. It was most likely during this time that he heard the call to foreign missions and subsequently set sail for the Far East.

Apparently, he arrived in the Straits Settlements sometime in 1836 and began his ministry on the Malayan Peninsula. Through schools, evangelism, and church work he shared the Gospel with both Chinese and Malays. His ministry at first was mainly located on the mainland directly across from the island of Penang. In 1845, he moved to Georgetown, Penang and continued serving there for the remainder of his life.

The well-known Christian, George Mueller, who established orphanages in England by faith alone influenced John George. When he went to the mission field, John George also carried on his ministries in this manner.

He was never appointed by any mission board and

never received a salary from any organization. No doubt he received love gifts from friends back in England and he owned property in Penang with many fruit trees, but it was his faith in God that provided for his daily needs and that of the work in which he was involved.

The first eight years of his time as a missionary John George lived as a bachelor. He was acquainted with other missionaries in the area and in time, God led him to marry one of them.

Samuel and Maria Dyer were missionaries serving in the area with the London Missionary Society. Samuel was a well-known Christian missionary who was vitally involved in preparing moveable type that could be used to print the Bible in the Chinese language. Unfortunately, in 1843 Samuel Dyer became ill and died leaving his widow, Maria, with three small children: Samuel, Burella, and Maria.

Because she too had a strong calling to mission work, Maria Dyer stayed on in the area running a girls' school. She arranged for her son, Samuel, to return to England for schooling but she kept her two daughters with her in Penang. It was not easy, however, for her to carry on in this way.

When John George Bausum saw how difficult it was for this widow he asked for her hand in marriage and she gratefully accepted. It is not for me to say whether they were "in love" or not but they both needed the stability and encouragement of a partner and felt it was God's will for them to unite forces.

Less than two years later, however, Maria passed away leaving John George a widower with two stepdaughters. He wrote on Maria's tombstone that she had "devoted her distinguished talents during the last 19 years of her life to the extension of Christ's kingdom among the Chinese females in the Straits..."

In correspondence with Maria's family in England and with the London Missionary Society, he arranged for Burella and Maria to return to England for their education. It must have been so difficult for John George then with an empty home, having tasted of the love and affection of both wife and children.

Serving at this time in the Southeast Asia area was a single woman missionary, **Jemima Poppy**. The Society for Promoting Female Education in the East had sent her from England as a missionary. We do not know much about her earlier background but judging from her later life she must have been a truly dedicated missionary.

Somehow, she and John George Bausum became acquainted and they were married on May 23, 1848 in Singapore. Five children were born to this marriage.

> Mary Elizabeth – 1849
> George Frederick – 1850
> William Henry – 1852
> Samuel Gottlieb – 1853
> Louisa Jane – 1855

Sadly, the last two children died in infancy and were buried in the same vault with Maria, John George's first wife.

Jemima was active in schoolwork, as was her husband, and in growing a local church. One hot day in August 1855, John George returned home after sitting up all night with a sick church member. He was very fatigued from the previous few days of ministry and became ill. After only a few hours of suffering great pain, he passed away in his beloved wife's arms. An autopsy revealed that one of the principle arteries of his heart had ruptured. John George was 43 years old. Like his first wife, Maria, he had served in the area for nineteen years before the Lord called him Home.

A missionary in her own right, Jemima continued her ministries and tried to oversee her husband's commitments as well. There were local helpers involved with the work but the heavy responsibilities added to her grief and caused her own health to fail. With three children to care for Jemima realized that she could not go on in this way.

She decided to sell the Bausum estate as well as the mission property and buildings. The Brethren Church bought the school and church buildings and continued the ministries that the Dyers and Bausums had begun. Another buyer bought the property with the fruit trees and Jemima packed up and left Penang.

All along, she had been in contact with her husband's stepdaughters, Burella and Maria Dyer. The girls had completed their education in England and had gone to Ningpo, China, to teach in a mission school planning to carry on their parents' commitment to mission work. They wrote to Jemima and suggested that she come to Ningpo and teach in that school so that is what Jemima decided to do.

Her children were still quite small so the four of them went by ship to Ningpo and established their home in that ancient city. There were already other missionaries serving there and the Bausums found love and fellowship as they adjusted to their new life without husband and father.

A single missionary named Miss Mary Ann Aldersey ran the girls' school where Jemima began to teach. This woman had a strong character and ruled both students and teachers with an iron hand. She took special care of the two Dyer sisters who were in their late teens. This proved to be a stumbling block to the relationship between Miss Aldersey and Jemima Poppy Bausum.

It was at this point in history that a young missionary named Hudson Taylor arrived in Ningpo with the vision to begin a missionary sending organization that later became the China Inland Mission. He was firmly convinced that to be an effective missionary going into the heart of China the foreigners should dress as the Chinese dressed even to the point of the men growing a queue as was the custom of

Chinese men in those days.

Hudson Taylor and Maria Dyer were strongly attracted to each other and he tried to court her. Miss Aldersey, however, looked upon this unusual missionary as not worthy of Maria's hand in marriage. Therefore, she did everything in her power to discourage and even block such a relationship from growing.

Jemima Bausum, on the other hand, saw true love budding and did what she could to encourage the young couple. She helped them pass notes back and forth and even arranged ways for them to meet for times to talk with one another.

As I mentioned above, this broke the relationship between Jemima and Miss Aldersey and, in time, Jemima felt obligated to leave that school. She went on to begin the first Baptist girls' school in Ningpo. When we visited Ningpo in 1991, it was our joy to locate this school, now a government school, and we found Mrs. Bausum's name a part of its recorded history as the founder.

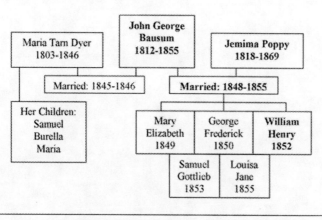

JOHN GEORGE BAUSUM FAMILY

LORD
CHINA

$\mathcal{M}$y great-grandfather, **Edward Clemens Lord**, was born in Carlisle, New York, on January 22, 1817. Brought up in a devout Christian home, he accepted the Lord Jesus as his personal Savior at the age of nineteen and went on to study theology. God called him into full time missionary service so the American Baptist Missionary Union appointed him in February 1846 to serve in China. He was ordained in August and married Lucy T. Lyon in September. The newly-weds sailed for China on January 5, 1847.

After months on the sea and a few weeks in Hong Kong, they traveled on to Shanghai and finally arrived on June 20 in Ningpo where their mission had asked them to settle. They had been traveling for five and one-half months! Since they found no suitable house in which to live, they proceeded to build a mission house while they also began language study. That first year was a busy time with many adjustments but a happy time for the Lords. On January 24, 1848 a son, Edward, was born to them and their letters home expressed great joy and thanksgiving to God.

By 1849, however, sickness and sorrow invaded their lives. Little one-and-one-half-year-old Eddie was taken ill and no medicine seemed effective. In a final effort to save his life, the family went on a boat trip at their doctor's advice - to give the child a "change of air." This proved unsuccessful, though, and on the night of October 5 the parents watched their little boy's life slip away.

One year later, Lucy gave birth to a baby girl who died within an hour. Lucy herself was already ill most of the time. Finally, in July 1851 the Lords boarded a ship and took a long quiet journey back to New York hoping that exposure to the sea air would strengthen Lucy's health. After three months at sea, she did seem to be stronger but then her health declined once more. On May 5, 1853 she died, attended by her loving husband and family in New York.

Shortly after this sad event, Dr. Lord married Lucy's younger sister, **Freelove Lyon**, and returned to Ningpo to continue his life's calling to share the Gospel with the Chinese. Freelove no doubt felt the same call and served faithfully beside her husband for the remaining seven years of her life. To this marriage was born five children. Sadly, Freelove died from inflammation of the lungs just twelve days after the birth of her fifth child. Dr. Lord, widowed for the second time, now had five small children to raise without a mother. This was a daunting prospect for him especially because of his deep involvement with the mission work. It was not long before he began looking for another wife.

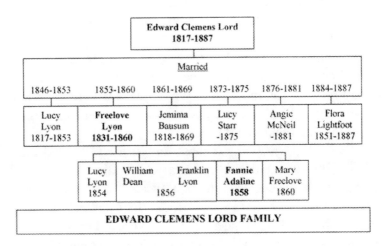

| Edward Clemens Lord ||||||
| 1817-1887 ||||||

Married					
1846-1853	1853-1860	1861-1869	1873-1875	1876-1881	1884-1887
Lucy Lyon 1817-1853	**Freelove Lyon 1831-1860**	Jemima Bausum 1818-1869	Lucy Starr -1875	Angie McNeil -1881	Flora Lightfoot 1851-1887

Lucy Lyon 1854	William Dean	Franklin Lyon 1856	**Fannie Adaline 1858**	Mary Freelove 1860

EDWARD CLEMENS LORD FAMILY

BAUSUM – LORD

CHINA

*J*emima Poppy Bausum, the widow of John George Bausum, had come to Ningpo, China, with her three small children in 1856. She taught in Miss Aldersey's school and served the Lord in every way possible. At some point in time, she decided to take her children to England where they stayed in a boarding school. Then she returned to Ningpo to continue her ministry.

Her daughter, Mary Elizabeth, adjusted to life in England and did well in her studies. The two sons did not do as well, perhaps because they were younger and because they were mischievous boys. The reports Jemima received about George Frederick and William Henry were troubling. To bring her sons back to Ningpo would greatly curtail her own mission activities but she feared what would happen to the boys if she left them in England. She began praying about what to do.

During this same period, Dr. E.C. Lord was widowed for the second time and trying to cope with five small children. He already knew Jemima Bausum and since both of them knew the pain and loneliness of being widowed, Dr. Lord asked Mrs. Bausum to marry him. She respected Dr. Lord as did all the missionaries serving in Ningpo, and she recognized that each of their ministries would benefit from a happier family life. Therefore, she consented to become the third Mrs. Lord in this way uniting the **Bausum and Lord** families. Since they both had small children and were facing difficulties regarding these children's education together they devised an ingenious plan.

Dr. Lord had a sister, Esther Lord McNeil, living in New York State. Perhaps Esther saw this as an opportunity to make her own contribution to foreign missions. At any rate, she agreed to help raise the five little MKs (missionary kids). Therefore, soon after their marriage in 1861, Jemima took her new husband's five children and sailed around the Cape of Africa and on to New York where she placed those precious lives in the care of their Aunt Esther. Then Jemima headed for England to get her own two sons. Bringing them to America, she also gave them over to Aunt Esther to grow up as brothers and sisters with the Lord children. Jemima then sailed back to Ningpo and never saw her sons again.

Mary Elizabeth Bausum, Jemima's daughter, stayed on in England and completed her education there. When she was seventeen years old, Mary traveled by ship along with Mr. and Mrs. Hudson Taylor (who was her stepsister, Maria Dyer) and a group of new missionaries to Ningpo to live and work with her mother. While living in Ningpo, Mary met and married one of Hudson Taylor's recruits, Stephen Paul Barchet. He was from Germany as Mary's father had been and they both felt a strong calling to missionary work in China. In fact, they made China their home, raised their own family there, and eventually died and were buried in Shanghai, China.

Meanwhile, **Jemima Poppy Bausum Lord** served alongside her second husband, Dr. E. C. Lord, for eight years until the Lord took her Home. We found a newspaper clipping in the Bausum family Bible. It was from a Fredonia, New York paper and told of Jemima's death. "Having…provided for the education of her children, she returned to her chosen work, and with untiring energy and zeal, engaged in the untried work of educating Chinese females; to do which she must contend with national prejudices....She successfully established a school of nearly fifty girls, for whom she acted as mother, in preparing their food, clothing, and education. Her school is now the largest and most successful in China..."

With Jemima's death, Dr. E.C. Lord was widowed for the third time. The long hard work of the mission field coupled with the loneliness of being separated from his own children led Dr. Lord to seek marital companionship three more times before his own death. Each of his wives was younger than her predecessor was but none of them lived for many years. Dr. Lord and his sixth wife both contracted cholera during an epidemic in 1887. She died just four days before her husband who was so ill that he never knew he had been widowed for the sixth time. Dr. Lord and five of his six wives were buried in Ningpo, China where he had served so faithfully for forty years.

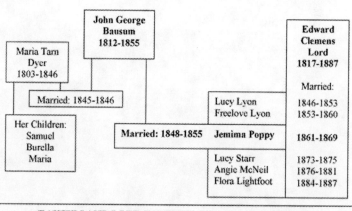

Maria Tam Dyer 1803-1846	John George Bausum 1812-1855		Edward Clemens Lord 1817-1887
			Married:
Married: 1845-1846		Lucy Lyon	1846-1853
		Freelove Lyon	1853-1860
Her Children: Samuel Burella Maria	Married: 1848-1855 Jemima Poppy		1861-1869
		Lucy Starr	1873-1875
		Angie McNeil	1876-1881
		Flora Lightfoot	1884-1887

BAUSUM AND LORD FAMILIES UNITED IN MARRIAGE

BAUSUM – LORD
AMERICA

*A*cross the ocean in Fredonia, New York, the **five Lord children** and **two Bausum boys** were growing up in Aunt Esther's home. That must have been an interesting situation as well as a challenging one for Esther McNeil. Together, there were four boys and three girls. Although their parents were married, the children were not related except through that marriage. Presumably, they got along well as brothers and sisters and no doubt formed normal sibling relationships in the process, with one exception.

Dr. E.C. Lord made a visit to America in 1874 and when he returned to Ningpo the next year he took his sixteen-year-old daughter Fannie with him. At this time, besides being a missionary Dr. Lord was serving as American Consul in Ningpo and Fannie worked as his secretary. After four years, she returned to America for her college education and then to be married.

We do not actually know whether the love affair began while they were living in Aunt Esther's home or after they had gone their separate ways. What we do know is that **William Henry Bausum** took **Fannie Adaline Lord** to be his bride on August 26, 1885. They were married in Chicago and then the young couple went west taking up a claim - a free grant of land from the government - and became ranchers in the Dakota Territory. It was a hard life, but I suppose those two MKs had learned to face many difficulties during their growing up years.

For the birth of their first child, Jennie June, Fannie returned to Chicago to have the convenience of city doctors. Her other six children, all boys, were born on the prairie. Having a daughter first proved to be of invaluable help to Fannie in the care of the younger siblings as well as with household chores. Mother and daughter grew very close.

Life on the prairie was hard, and the family faced great sadness, especially when the two youngest children died suddenly from unnamed illnesses. Fannie and William had a strong faith, though, and continued to trust God and raise their surviving children to trust Him, also.

William Bausum was a rancher focusing on sheep, although he also raised cattle, horses and the inevitable chickens and pigs. Even as Jennie June was a help to her mother in the house, the brothers who came after her were of valuable help to their father on the ranch. With hard ground and not much rain, the ranchers in Dakota worked long difficult days to make ends meet. Unfortunately, this meant the older boys were more often on the ranch than in the schoolhouse.

There was a one-room school about half a mile from the Bausum house but only Jennie and the younger boys were able to attend on a regular basis. My father, Robert Lord Bausum, could recall walking to that school and sitting just in front of his big sister Jennie from the time he was five years old until the family moved east.

Education for the younger boys was one of the many reasons William and Fannie finally decided to give up ranching and move to Maryland. Mary Bausum, William's sister, and her husband Stephen Barchet had purchased a farm near Annapolis, Maryland. Although they continued to make their home in China most of the time, one of their sons was living on the family farm. William and Fannie corresponded with him and arranged to stay with the Barchets until they were able to buy their own farm and get it up and running.

Moving the family of seven, along with all their furniture and farm animals, was quite an undertaking. In March 1905, two sons left by train taking household furnishings and the five horses they had decided to keep. Then Fannie, Jennie and Robert left by passenger train making a memorable visit to ninety-three year old Aunt Esther in New York. Then they traveled on to Maryland.

The third and final part of the move was not until July. William and one son, Fred, had stayed to sell the ranch and settle accounts. Finally, they left by freight train with a carload of milk cows. When they reached Cumberland, Maryland, the train stopped and William went to buy some food. He was crossing the tracks returning to the freight train when a passenger train swept around a curve and killed him instantly. What a terrible blow for Fannie and the children!

Fortunately, the teenaged daughter and two older sons had plenty of experience on the South Dakota ranch. In time, Fannie was able to purchase some land and with the help of her children, she got a dairy farm up and running. The two younger boys were able to continue their schooling although they also had to help with the work. In 1913, tragedy again struck this family when the beloved daughter and sister, Jennie, died from abscesses which would not respond to available medications. Yet God used that great sorrow to draw them all closer to Him - especially Robert.

He had finished high school and was working in Baltimore at the time of Jennie's death. As he processed this tremendous loss, Robert began to understand that God was calling him into the Gospel ministry. With encouragement from his pastor and family, Robert resigned from his job and entered the University of Richmond.

He heard the challenge of foreign missions during this

time and committed his life to that end. After three years at the university, Robert decided a university degree was just a piece of paper so he moved on to Crozer Seminary in Chester, Pennsylvania, for his theological training and final preparations for becoming a missionary.

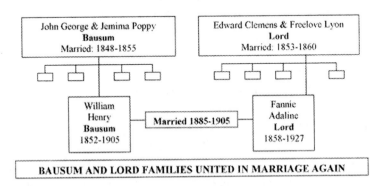

BAUSUM AND LORD FAMILIES UNITED IN MARRIAGE AGAIN

BAUSUM

CHINA

*W*hile in school, **Robert Lord Bausum** pastored several churches. When the days of preparation were done, he applied to the Southern Baptist Foreign Mission Board and they appointed him to China, the land where his ancestors had served. He did not go to Ningpo, however, but to a city in southern China called Kweilin.

In August 1920, he said good-bye to family and friends and traveled by train across America and up through Canada to Vancouver where along with other missionaries he boarded the SS Empress of Japan to cross the Pacific Ocean. After an interesting voyage, the ship docked in Shanghai for a few days and Robert was able to visit his aunt, Mary Elizabeth Bausum Barchet, who was still living and active in the church life there. The ship then continued on to Hong Kong where Robert left it and boarded a river steamer to Wuchow. Finally, he traveled by houseboat to Kweilin and arrived in September 1920. He began language study and ministry almost immediately.

Like his grandfathers before him, Robert soon was active in education as principal of the Chu Chai Boys' School, as well as participating in evangelism and church life. He was involved in building both a new school building and a missionary residence. Those first years were a time of learning many new things.

In 1921, his mother Fannie Lord Bausum came to China to take care of her son as well as teach missionary children who lived on the Baptist compound. Having spent four years between high school and college with her father, Dr. E. C. Lord, in Ningpo Fannie was pleased to return to the land of her birth to help once more in missionary efforts. Unfortunately, it was a time of turmoil in China as Communism was just beginning to rear its ugly head. This put a great strain on Fannie's health. In 1926, Robert brought her back to America and she passed away just before Christmas 1927. In the late summer of 1928, Robert returned to China for his second missionary term and a brand new adventure.

Four years into Robert's first term in China, a single lady missionary had arrived in Kweilin from Texas. **Euva Evelyn Majors** almost immediately became principal of the Pei Tseng Girls School. While Robert was in America on his first furlough, she helped oversee his boys' school and they often corresponded regarding school issues. As Fannie lay dying, she encouraged her son Robert to look for a wife and she mentioned Euva specifically. Robert had also reached the decision that being single was not God's plan for him so, when he returned to China in 1928 he began to court Euva. They were soon engaged to be married.

Immediately a problem arose. The other missionaries felt it was not "proper" for an engaged couple to be living and working together in such close proximity so Euva was sent back to Texas for a mini-furlough. During those six months, she enjoyed visiting family and friends as well as preparing for her wedding. When she sailed back to China, Robert met the ship in Hong Kong and the couple was married there in the Union Church on July 23, 1929. They boarded the same ship and traveled on to the Philippines for a month-long honeymoon. Then they returned to Kweilin as a "properly" married couple and continued their ministries as before.

Two years later, Robert and Euva were excitedly awaiting the birth of their first child. However, when the time of birth arrived there was no missionary doctor in Kweilin so an English woman doctor attended Euva. Unfortunately, her medical skills were not very advanced and the healthy baby girl died at birth.

The stricken couple named her Carolyn Ruth and buried her in the flower garden near the house Robert had built. Over the next two years, the Lord blessed their home with two sons: George Robert and Howard Thomas. Four years later came the daughter they had longed for – me – and they named me Dorothy Lord Bausum.

My parents served in Kweilin through most of World War II helping the Chinese people through that terrible experience. After an extended furlough in Baltimore, Maryland, they were able to return to Taiwan in 1951 for their final term of overseas service.

My brothers were already in college but since I was only fourteen years old, they took me with them to Taiwan. I went "kicking and screaming" but the Lord used that experience to confirm my own calling to foreign missions. Robert and Euva retired in 1958 and had seven years of productive ministry sharing all over America about foreign missions.

Then Euva developed cancer and died in September 1966 after an eleven-month battle with that dreaded disease. Robert continued to travel around the USA sharing about missions until he died in an automobile accident. He was eighty-six years old and he "died with his boots on" as he was on a trip sharing about missions, even then.

Looking back over my parents', grandparents', and great-grandparents' lives I am again awed and humbled at their faithfulness to the call to "go into all the world and preach the gospel..." It was my privilege also, to hear that call and to have a small part in that same kind of ministry.

"Lord, you have assigned me my portion and my cup;
you have made my lot secure.
The boundary lines have fallen for me in pleasant places;
surely I have a delightful inheritance."

Psalm 16:5-6

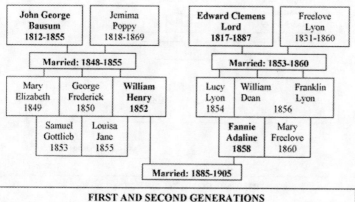

FIRST AND SECOND GENERATIONS

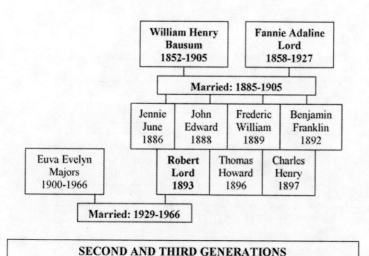

SECOND AND THIRD GENERATIONS

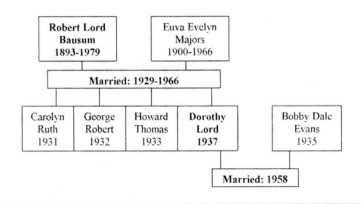

THIRD AND FOURTH GENERATIONS

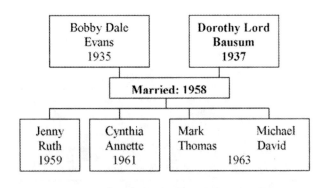

FOURTH AND FIFTH GENERATIONS

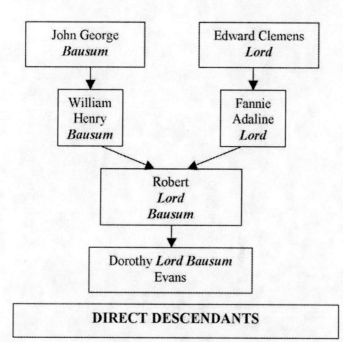

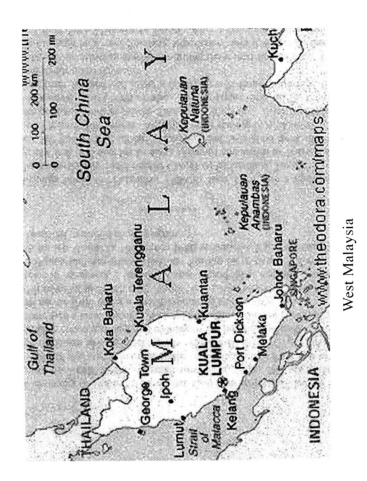

West Malaysia

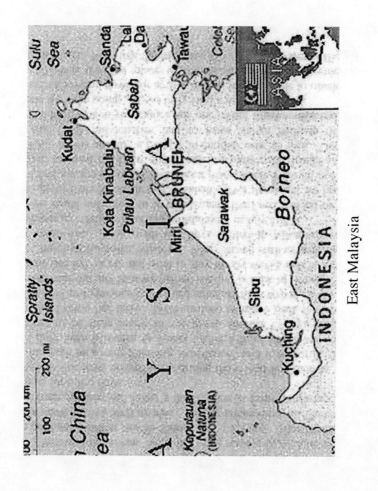

East Malaysia

China

Printed in the United States
119847LV00002B/130-351/A